The Power Of Human Speech
In The Jewish Tradition

Edited and Compiled By

Rabbi Dov Peretz Elkins

Winner of the National Jewish Book Award

Mazo Publishers

The Power Of Human Speech
Copyright © 2020 Dov Peretz Elkins

ISBN 978-1-946124-66-1

Contact The Author
DPE@jewishgrowth.org

Mazo Publishers
Chaim Mazo, Publisher
Website: www.mazopublishers.com
Email: mazopublishers@gmail.com

Front cover image by Thomas Wolter

54321

Every reasonable effort has been made to trace the authors of the articles included in this book to attribute credit, but if any have been inadvertently overlooked, be in contact so that due credit may be acknowledged in future editions.

No part of this publication may be translated, reproduced, stored in a retrieval system, or transmitted in any form or by any means, electronic, mechanical, photocopying, recording or otherwise, without prior permission in writing from the publisher.

In Appreciation of

The Dedicated Contributions of

The Clark-Siegel Family

To the State of Israel

To Peace

and to Jewish People everywhere.

Contents

Contributors	7
The Author	8
Rambam's Five Categories of Speech	10
Quotables	11

Part One ~ 15
Leshon Hatov – Speaking Positively

Leshon Hatov: A Great Mitzvah	16
Affirm Others	17
Affirmation is an Attitude	18
Family First	20
It's Okay to be Affirmed	21
God, Too, Loves Praise	22
The Elderly, the Family	23
The Seventh Gate	24
A Voice Inside My Head	25
A Prayer	26
Words Can Kill	27
Say A Nice Thing	28
Changing For The Better	28
No Wrong Time to Say the Right Thing	29
Leshon Hara and *Leshon Hatov* – Positive Speech	30
Leshon Hatov – Healing with Words	32
Positive Words	33
Speech In The Positive	34

Part Two ~ 35
Leshon Hara – Negative Speech

Permissible *Leshon Hara*	36
Biblical Speech	36
Signs	39
The Iron Dome Against *Leshon Hara*	40
Avoiding *Leshon Hara* – Messages	45
Just Talkin'	46
Like An Arrow	48
Words That Wound	48

The Power To Speak	49
Put Your *Yetzer Hara* In Its Place	50
To Vex With Words	51
Even If True – Gossip Is Still A Sin	53
For the Sin of *Leshon Hara*	55
The Power of Words	56
Be Careful Of Unnecessary Words!	56
Of What Importance Can Mere "Words" Be?	57
Care With Words, Speech And Prayer	57
Gossip: Where Do We Start When We Want To Stop?	58
Judaism Is, Above All, A Love of Language	58
Resist The Temptation	59
Undermining Society	61
Tracking Words Is Harder Than Tracking Money	61
Tale Bearing And Evil Gossip	62
When Children Learn To Talk	63
The Twisted Kernel Of Truth	64
A Difficult Law To Obey	64
Words Are More Like An Arrow Than A Sword	65
Words Are Holy	66
The Terrible Gossiper	68
Death and Life are in the "Hand" of the Tongue	69
Positive Word Power	78
The Leprosy Of Irresponsible Speech	80
Things God Hates	80
Sensitivity To Speech	81
The Drive-By Sin	84
Smooth and Deceptive Language	85
Rumors: Is It Appropriate to Pass One On?	85
Our Weapons Of War	87
The Local Gossip Queen	88
Uncontrolled Appetites	88
Metzora: Slander and its Comeuppance	91
Guard That Which Comes Out Of Your Mouth	93
The Power Of Words	93
The Greatest Sin – Sinning Against One's People	94
Feathers in the Wind	94
Listening and Filtering	96
Guard Your Tongue	96

Guard That Which Enters And Leaves Your Mouth	98
Meet the Evil Inclination	98
Rumor Has It	99
Shmirat Halashon – Avoiding Gossip	101
The Tongue As Sword	104
When Words Don't Amount To Anything	106
Gossip And Talking About Others	107
Speech – Use It, Don't Abuse It	109
The Power of Thought and Speech	110
Soft Words	110
Speak No Evil	112
Thought, Speech, and Action	115
Words That Help, Words That Heal	117
The Tongue Set Free?	117
Spiritual Toxicity	118
Use Your Words	119
How to Use Your Most Powerful Weapon	121
The Toothpaste Sacrifice	122
Gossip Is Not Harmless	123
When Words Hurt	124
Electronic Leshon Hara	125
Your Word Is Your Bond	127
Creating Your World Through Language	128

Part Three ~ 131
Misusing Speech

How Words Lose their Meaning	132
Words, Just Words	133

Part Four ~ 141
The Sound Of Silence

The Eloquence Of Silence	142
Knowing When To Remain Silent	145
The Sound Of Silence	147
The Path Of Silence And The Path Of Words	149
The Power Of Silence	152

Glossary ~ 158

Contributors

R. Kassel Abelson	51
R. Marc D. Angel	125, 132
R. Bradley Artson	48, 80
Dr. Erica Brown	96, 99, 104, 110
Irving M. Bunim	50
Chofetz Chaim (R. Yisrael M. Kagan)	23, 55
R. Aryeh Citron	36
R. Jordan D. Cohen	81
R. Seymour J. Cohen	56
R. Dianne Cohler-Esses	128
Kirk Douglas	64
R. Yechiel Eckstein	30, 32, 94, 96, 118
Thomas Edison	106
R. Elimelekh of Lizhensk	26
R. Dov Peretz Elkins	16, 28, 59, 152
R. Ari Enkin	28
R. Natan Fenner	119
Dr. Stanley Friedland	61
R. Jonathan Ginsburg	62
R. Yoel Glick	149
R. Prof. David Golinkin	69
Steve Goodier	29
R. Michael Gold	88, 147
R. Sidney Greenberg	66
R. Joshua Hammerman	101
R. Yael Hammerman	121
R. Abraham J. Heschel	142
Jeff Jacoby	63
R. Yisroel Jungreis	33, 36, 98, 127
R. Chaim Listfield	28
R. Ya'aqob Menashe	87
R. Pinchas Peli	45
R. Zelig Pliskin	78
R. Michael Rascoe	133
R. Jack Riemer	46
R. Shlomo Riskin	53
R. Donald B. Rossoff	65
R. Ephraim Rubinger	49
R. Jonny Sack	40
R. Eli Scheller	98, 109
R. Ismar Schorsch	58
R. Ariel Sholklapper	115
Chaya Shuchat	112
Moshe Sokolow	91
R. Kerrith Solomon	124
R. Pesach Dahvid Stadlin	24, 25
R. Joseph Telushkin	48, 85, 107, 117
R. Alissa Thomas-Newborn	122
R. Avi Weiss	145
R. David Wolpe	84, 117

The Author

Dov Peretz Elkins is a nationally known lecturer, educator, workshop leader, author, and book critic. He is a popular speaker on the Jewish circuit.

Rabbi Elkins is a recipient of the National Jewish Book Award, and is the author of over 53 books. His *Chicken Soup For The Jewish Soul* was on the NY Times bestseller list.

Among Rabbi Elkins' other books are *Rosh Hashanah Readings: Inspiration, Information and Contemplation, Yom Kippur Readings,* and *The Wisdom of Judaism: An Introduction to the Values of the Talmud.*

His most recent books are *To Climb The Rungs – Memoirs of a Rabbi* (Mazo Publishers), *Jewish Stories from Heaven and Earth: Inspiring Tales to Nourish the Heart and Soul, Tales of the Righteous, Simple Actions for Jews to Help Green the Planet, Heart and Scroll: Inspiring Stories from the Masters* (Mazo Publishers), *In the Spirit: Insights for Spiritual Renewal in the 21st Century, For Those Left Behind: A Jewish Anthology of Comfort and Healing* (Mazo Publishers) and *A Treasury of Thoughts on Israel and Zionism* (Mazo Publishers). See other books by Dov Peretz Elkins at www.jewishgrowth.org.

Rabbi Elkins served in several outstanding congregations in Rochester, NY, Cleveland, OH, and in Princeton, NJ, before retirement. He earned a doctorate in pastoral counseling in Rochester, NY.

Dr. Elkins lives in Jerusalem with his wife, Maxine (Miryam). They have six children and twelve grandchildren.

> לֹא תֵלֵךְ רָכִיל בְּעַמֶּיךָ
>
> *Do not go around as a talebearer among your people.*
> Leviticus 19:16

Rambam's Five Categories of Speech

- **Required Speech,** such as the reading and study of Torah, a Biblical command.

- **Forbidden Speech,** such as false testimony, lies, gossip, curses, and vulgarity.

- **Repulsive Speech,** that is neither beneficial not harmful, like most chatter of the masses about the news, the customs of such-and-such a king in his palace, the circumstances of the death of so-and-so, or how so-and-so became rich. The Sages called such speech "idle chatter" and the extremely pious strove to omit all such talk from their conversations. It was said of Rav that an idle comment never passed his lips all his life.

- **Desirable Speech,** that inspires the soul toward higher ideals and discourages it from the reverse through stories and songs. Such speech includes the glorification of men of character and the disparagement of shallowness.

- **Permitted Speech,** which is necessary for business, food and drink, clothing, etc. It is in this category that we are to minimize our words, since the other negative categories should be shunned entirely while the positive categories should be embraced.

The Biblical format of prayer is as follows: a person should first relate the praise of God, and secondly ask for their needs as a supplication, and conclude with thanks to God for the good that has been bestowed upon them, each person according to their ability.

Rambam (Maimonides)
Laws of Prayer Chapter 1, Law 2

Quotables

What is noble can be expressed in any tongue. What is ignoble should be said in no tongue.
Maimonides

Feeling gratitude and not expressing it is like wrapping a present and not giving it.
William Arthur Ward
Teacher, Author and Editor

Think three times before you speak.
Maurice Hollinger, z'l
Grandfather of the publisher of this book

Every word that doesn't increase the light of God contributes to the darkness. People are so concerned about what they put into their mouths; if only we were as careful with what comes out.
Mother Teresa

The saddest thing in the world is that we know so much about each other's mistakes, but how much do we know about each other's good deeds? How much do we know about each other's good points?
Rabbi Shlomo Carlebach

Take care of your thoughts when you are alone, take care of your words when you are with others.
Anonymous

If you hear an evil thing, bury it seven cubits deep.
Ahiqar 2, 54

If you hear anything, let it die with you; be strong and it will not split you.
Ben Sira 19:10

Gossip is liked, but its monger is hated.
Shlomo Rubin, Sefer Ha-middot

It could be that I might enjoy talking about and listening to the intimate details of other people's lives, and discussing other people's character flaws, but I can't even go there, since my Heavenly Father has forbidden this kind of speech.
Anonymous

If you believe all gossip around you, you will be left without one good friend.
Immanuel of Rome, Mahbarot

It is the way of the slanderer to begin with praises and end with obloquy.
Tanhuma, Sh'lah

The slanderer who looks for faults is like the fly that only settles on a dirty place.
Orhot Tsaddiqim, Sha'ar l'shon ha-ra

Who slanders others for their guilt will be damned in return for his innocence.
Hunen Ibn Itshaq, Mussar Ha-pilosphim

Who slanders others for what they are innocent of will be damned for his own guilt.
Mishlei Hakhamim

If a horse with four legs can sometimes stumble, how much more a human with only one tongue.
Sholom Aleichem

A lie gets halfway around the world before the truth has a chance to get its pants on.
Winston Churchill

The wise person, even when he holds his tongue, says more than the fool when he speaks.
Yiddish Proverb

Everything thought is not meant to be said.
The Kotzker Rebbe

The soul, like the body, lives by what it feeds on.
Josiah Gilbert Holland

One who speaks an evil word of an absent man or woman is not welcome at this table.
Author Unknown

Some people have trouble knowing the difference between saying what's on their mind and minding what they say.
Unknown

By swallowing evil words unsaid, no one has ever harmed his stomach.
Unknown

Two angels in heaven are seated before telephone switchboards.

One switchboard is entitled "Requests" and that angel cannot keep up with the numerous calls.

The other switchboard is entitled "Calls of Appreciation" and that switchboard is covered with cobwebs as the angel sleeps – nary a call.

Part One

Leshon Hatov – Speaking Positively

Part One

Leshon Hatov: A Great Mitzvah
Rabbi Dov Peretz Elkins

In one of his novels, the Russian author Ivan Turgenev presents the following dialogue:

> *I was once walking in the street when a beggar stopped me. He was a frail old man, with inflamed eyes, blue chapped lips, filthy rough rags and disgusting sores. Oh how poverty had disfigured this repulsive creature!*
>
> *He stretched out to me his red, swollen, filthy hand and whimpered for alms. I reached into my pocket, but no wallet, no coins, no money did I find. I had left them all at home.*
>
> *The beggar waited, and his outstretched hand twitched and trembled slightly. Embarrassed and confused I seized his hand and pressed it and said: "Brother, don't be angry with me. I am sorry but I have nothing to give you. I left my wallet at home, brother."*
>
> *The beggar raised his bloodshot eyes to mine. His blue lips smiled and he returned the pressure of my fingers. "Never mind," he stammered. "Thank you, thank you for this, for this too was a gift. No one ever called me brother before."*

It's a touching slice of narrative through which we see a whole lifetime: a beggar who has probably been mistreated and deprived of love most of his life, hungry, tired, desperate for a handout, a few simple coins, and he doesn't even get that. What he does receive is much more valuable. How simple it is to call one our brother or sister, to express a word of love or support to one in emotional need. Yet we rush through life, eyes narrowly focused on the task, hurrying to finish our chores, afraid to take the emotional risk of opening ourselves up to our neighbor, and the kind word goes unexpressed.

In the Great Confessional of Yom Kippur, we list many sins, one of which states, "Al chet she-hatanu lefanekha bedibbur peh" – for the sin we have committed before You by the words of our mouths. Sometimes that sin is the expression of a negative word, a nasty comment, a harsh phrase, a cruel joke, or a sarcastic remark. At other times that sin is committed by refraining from a positive remark.

Benjamin Franklin reminded us that there are two sides to the power of speech when he wrote, "Speak ill of no man, but speak all the good you know of everybody."

Our tradition uses the phrase *Leshon Hara* to refer to evil speech – slander, gossip, put-downs, vilification of any kind – a nasty, evil, and pernicious act that can destroy a reputation and ruin a life. One-fourth of all the sins listed in the Great Confessional touch on *Leshon Hara*. However, the other side of the coin is equally important: what I choose to call *Leshon Hatov*.

Leshon Hatov means verbal affirmation of another person, the careful use of words which our tradition implies when it warns us about the sins of speech, of *dibbur peh*. It is what the ancient Greek writer, Cicero, referred to when he said that "the sweetest of all sound is praise."

Affirm Others

Sometimes we are afraid to praise others. We think praise will "go to their heads", or that they will be embarrassed. Yet if we think about it carefully, we could wish that we were as careful about praise and compliments as we are careless about gossip and put-downs. No one I know ever died from being appreciated. But many people have been saved from despair and hopelessness by a kind word properly spoken.

The Book of Proverbs, one of the finest collections of wisdom regarding human relationships, contains sage aphorisms about the importance of words of encouragement:

Pleasant words are like a honeycomb,
> sweet to the palate and cure for the body. (16:24)

Care in the heart of a man bows it down,
> but a good word makes it glad. (12:25)

Do not withhold good from one who deserves it,
> when you have the power to say it. (3:27)

In the last chapter of the Biblical book we find the *Eshet Chayil*, that beautiful poem of praise recited by devoted husbands each

Part One

Friday night at the Shabbat dinner table, in which we read: "The children of the woman of valor rise up and call her blessed, and her husband praises her, saying, 'Many women have done well, but you surpass them all'" (31:28, 29).

In the prayers chanted in the daily *Shacharit* service, a selection from Exodus is quoted (14:31): "And when Israel saw the wondrous power which the Lord had wielded against the Egyptians, the people feared the Lord, and they had faith in the Lord and His servant Moshe." The verse continues, "Then sang Moshe," which, the commentaries explain, means that only when the people had faith in Moshe could he sing.

Turgenev's beggar lacked a song in his life because no one had faith in him. Only when we feel the faith, trust, and encouragement of loved ones can we continue our important tasks and achieve our highest potential. There is something powerful in the praise and appreciation of significant people in our lives that holding it back becomes one of the most harmful wedges in any relationship. "The supreme happiness in life," wrote Victor Hugo, "is the conviction that we are loved." *Al chet she-hatanu lefanekha bedibbur peh* – for the sin which we committed before you with our mouths. The words which we say, and the words we refrain from saying.

Affirmation is an Attitude

What I am saying about words of affirmation and appreciation sounds reasonable enough. So why do we not offer them more frequently? A good psychologist would find many reasons. One of them is that our words are a reflection of our attitude toward people. If our attitudes are positive and constructive, then we will have less difficulty expressing affirmation and praise. In addition, to be happier in their relationships people need to "catch people" doing right more often. This tendency of looking for the good in life and in people will assist us in expressing nice things. We say only what we first see. If we see the good, we will better be able to express it.

Our tradition is full of examples of the need to look positively at others. Several centuries ago, Maimonides addressed this concept in the *Mishneh Torah* (Code of Jewish Law): "A wise person gives everyone a friendly greeting, judges all people favorably, loves peace and strives for it, so that all are kindly toward him. He dwells on the merits of his fellow man, without ever disparaging him" (Sefer Hamada 5:7).

To the Hasidic masters, the only way to look upon another Jew was to do so with a positive mental attitude, and to judge others *lechaf zechut* – with a presumption of merit. The classic illustration of a positive attitude is that of Rabbi Levi Yitzchak of Berditchev. One Yom Kippur, Reb Levi saw a fellow Jew smoking a cigarette. "Surely," said the Rabbi, "you have forgotten that this is Yom Kippur!" "No," said the man, "I know that today is Yom Kippur." "Surely," continued Reb Levi, "you are not aware that the Jewish law codes forbid smoking on Yom Kippur." "No," said the man, "I know that it is forbidden to smoke on Yom Kippur." "Then surely," pursued Reb Levi Yitzchak, "your doctor told you that because of your nerves, you have to smoke on Yom Kippur." "No," continued the Jew, "I know it's Yom Kippur, I know I shouldn't smoke on Yom Kippur, my doctor did not advise me to smoke, I'm just smoking!" "What a wonderful Jew," reacted Reb Levi, "three times I gave him a chance to lie, and he still tells the truth!"

Another story is told of a wealthy Hasid, a diamond merchant, who was listening to his rebbe, Shalom Ber of Lubavitch, praising some of the townspeople. "But Rebbe," argued the Hasid, "why do you make such a fuss over these simpletons?" "Because they have many special qualities," answered the teacher. "Well, I just can't see them," responded the Hasid. Later in the discussion, the rebbe asked to see some of the Hasid's precious diamonds. The gem merchant was delighted to have the opportunity to impress his teacher, and, pointing to a particularly valuable stone, he said to the rebbe, "This one is something really special!" "But I can't see anything in it," said the rebbe. The gem merchant explained to his teacher, "You must be a connoisseur to know how to look at diamonds." The rebbe then said, "But every person is also truly something special. You just have to be a connoisseur to know how to look at him!"

Rabbi Israel Salanter, well-known founder of the *Musar* Movement (the 19th century effort to center people's attention on ethical responsibilities), explains that God gave us two eyes so that with one we can look at our neighbor, focusing on virtues, and

Part One

with the other, we are to turn inward to see our own shortcomings in order to correct them.

Family First

The most tragic thing about our failure to affirm is that this happens most with those who most need our affirmation: our family. No one needs love, attention, and appreciation more than a child from a parent, a wife from her husband, a husband from his wife. Yet somehow the family is where we fail most often. Every Rabbi has stories of funerals at which he/she officiates, and during which time he/she praises the deceased with the fitting words of a eulogy. Then, someone in the family approaches and says, "You know, Rabbi, there were so many times when I wanted to say words of kindness and love, but I just could not get them out of my mouth." In the words of George Eliot, "I like not only to be loved, but to be told that I am loved; the realm of silence is large enough beyond the grave."

We neglect our children the same way. Children need encouragement and positive reinforcement for their normal growth and development. They need it the same way they need proper nutrition to make their bones get stronger and their bodies grow properly. What William James said over a half a century ago applies with no more force than it does to our children: "The deepest principle of human nature is the craving to be appreciated."

One of the most beautiful customs in our tradition is the blessing by parents of their children on Shabbat eve and before Kol Nidre on Yom Kippur eve. We know that our children do many things that anger and frustrate us. Yet when it comes to the Shabbat blessing, we put aside those negative feelings, and turn our thoughts and words only to pleasant prayers and positive hopes.

In the Torah, when both Isaac and Jacob bless their children,[1] we are told that "the eyes of the aging patriarchs were dimmed for age, so that they could not see." Why, ask the commentators, is it said of both that their eyes are dimmed? This is to inform us that

---

1   Genesis 27:1, 48:10.

when blessing our children, we should shut our eyes and not see their flaws, only their good points.[2]

Psychologist Erik Erikson warns us that "the most deadly of all sins is the mutilation of a child's spirit."

An ancient Chinese proverb tells us that a child's life is like a piece of paper on which every passerby leaves a mark. We can add that the mark of a parent is the most potent of all.

Somehow, when relationships are most strongly solidified, such as with family members, it is hardest to break through that emotional barrier and share our deepest feelings of love and caring. While accomplishing this goal requires the most courage, the satisfaction is greatest. Nowhere are acts of affirmation more desperately needed to produce healthy marriages, children, and families than in the home.

It's Okay to be Affirmed

One of the barriers we must transcend in the process of learning how to offer love and appreciation is to accept that we all need such affirmation. Needing others to care about us is not a sign of weakness or immaturity; rather, it is a deep universal human need, and the sooner we recognize it, the easier it will be to accept praise from others. From time to time we discover that some strong, powerful, or heroic figure exposes his or her own personal need for appreciation, and it touches us. We are touched because we (wrongly) assumed all along that strong people did not have these needs.

After President Lincoln's assassination, a number of items were found in his pockets, including eight newspaper clippings lauding his accomplishments. The historian reporting this comments, "Here was a man who withstood brutal verbal abuse without flinching, but when he found an article that praised him, he kept it. Even to a casual reader these eight articles are heart-warming. The contents of Lincoln's pockets have an immediacy that transcends time. They invoke a sad, thoughtful and even vulnerable man." [3]

To all those who believe that praise and appreciation only serve

---

2   Cf. Shmuel Yosef Agnon, *Days of Awe*, p. 171.
3   NY Times, 3-29-86.

Part One

to make one vain, think of Abe Lincoln. Rather than make one vain, *Leshon Hatov* sustains us, uplifts us, and strengthens us. In the words of the British playwright, James Barrie, "The praise that comes of love does not make us vain, but humble rather."

God, Too, Loves Praise

For skeptics who are still unconvinced that the goal of affirming our loved ones is valid, we have one more important piece of evidence. Turn through the leaves of the sacred Book of Psalms and you will find that praise of God is one of the highest forms of prayer. Not only does the Psalmist urge our frequent and melodious praise of God, but God Himself, in the 50th Psalm, asks for it, in these words: "Whoever offers Me thanks and praise, honors me."[4]

The prominent Christian theologian C.S. Lewis asks the obvious question: Why is there so much praise of God in the Psalms? He explains that for a long time he had a hard time accepting the idea that God was so vain so as to ask for compliments from His creatures. Finally, he realized why.

The world rings with praise ... readers (praising) their favorite poet, walkers praising the countryside, players praising their favorite game – praise of weather, wines, dishes, actors, motors, horses, colleges. ... I had not noticed how the humblest, and at the same time most balanced and capacious minds praised most, while the cranks, misfits and malcontents praised least.

I had not noticed either that just as men spontaneously praise whatever they value, so they spontaneously urge us to join them in praising it: "Isn't she lovely? Wasn't it glorious? Don't you think that magnificent?" The Psalmists in telling everyone to praise God are doing what all men do when they speak of what they care about. I think we delight to praise what we enjoy because the praise not merely expresses but completes the enjoyment; it is its appointed consummation. It is not out of compliment that lovers keep on telling one another how beautiful they are; the delight is incomplete till it is expressed.[5]

In sum, if we love, then we must praise that which we love.

---

4   Psalm 50:23.
5   C.S. Lewis, *Reflections on the Psalms*.

If we do not love, then we are dead, spiritually if not physically. Giving and receiving unconditional love are the sum of all that we are, and by doing so we affirm those whom we love in the deepest possible way. It is the heart of who we are as human beings and as creatures of God.

May God always give us the gift, and the strength to use it: to love, to share, and to receive, and thus to enlarge our hearts and our capacity for a fuller and deeper life.

The Elderly, the Family
Chofetz Chaim (Rabbi Yisrael Meir Kagan)

If someone were to speak *Leshon Hara* about an elderly person, he would be violating the mitzvah of "In the presence of the elderly you shall rise",[6] which teaches us to treat our elders with respect and honor. Certainly, says the Chofetz Chaim, *Leshon Hara* demonstrates a lack of respect. If the subject of *Leshon Hara* is a Torah scholar one violates the commandment to honor a *Talmid Hacham*,[7] "show deference to the old," and may, in certain circumstances, be guilty of actual heresy. If the victim of *Leshon Hara* is a Kohen then the positive commandment of "and you must treat them as holy" which teaches us to treat Kohanim with added respect, has also been transgressed.[8]

We know that people often act toward those outside their family circle with more respect than they show toward the members of their own family. Many Torah sources stress that the true barometer of a person's behavior is not how he treats people when the world is watching, but how he treats his family in the privacy of his home. Unfortunately, in some homes, ridicule plays a big part in family interaction. Sometimes, God forbid, a parent is the victim of these barbs, especially when the children are married and their parents are not present to hear their comments. The *Yetzer Hara* (evil inclination) has a very effective method for opening the door to this type of *Leshon Hara*. He says, "Maybe you can refrain from speaking *Leshon Hara* outside the home, but the boundaries of *Shmirat Halashon* (guarding one's speech) stop at

---

6   Kiddushin 31b / Leviticus 19:32.
7   Ibid.
8   Vayikra 21:8.

your front door. Within the family, people are close and contact is constant, and *Shmirat Halashon* is all but impossible."

The Chofetz Chaim teaches that speaking negatively of an older sibling, a step-parent or, God forbid, a father or mother, is not only *Leshon Hara,* it is a violation of the commandment, Honor your father and mother.[9] There is also a curse applied to children who show parents disrespect: Cursed is one who insults his father or mother.[10]

One of the primary reasons Hashem created the family unit was so that it could be a workshop, a place for the *neshamah* (soul) to develop. The home is where we learn to be less self-centered, where we develop a love of *Chesed* (kindness) towards others. When the laws of *Shmirat Halashon* guide the family's interactions, each *neshamah* which this "workshop" produces can develop to its full, rich potential.

The Seventh Gate
Rabbi Pesach Dahvid Stadlin

The mouth is the only opening on the face that one can completely control what comes in and out of it. Most humans have seven primary gates on their heads that connect us to the outside physical world. From the outside in, we have two ears, two eyes, two nose apertures, and one mouth. Seven gates. Seven portals. The Torah tells us we are to place righteous judges and diligent enforcers by our gates.[11]

Amazing! Yes! We are to be conscious of who or what we co-resonate with, what we let in, what we let out, which billboards we stare at, which words bathe our being. Your life and your being are the most sacred things we have. Let's fill them with beauty!

But realistically, we cannot always control what we hear. And we cannot always choose what we see. And smells can drift their way on the wind, past the guards, and without our judges ever having decided. The mouth stands alone. It is the only gate on our head of which we can completely be the master. We can have total jurisdiction over which words we let out. We can also be totally in

---

9 Exodus 20:12.
10 Deuteronomy 27:16.
11 Deuteronomy 16:18.

charge of what food and drink we let in.

Now picture the golden Menorah in the heart of the Temple in Jerusalem. Picture it sitting there right next to the Holy of Holies, represented by a *Ner Tamid,* an eternal light, that still shines in the world today! The Menorah had six ornately decorated branches of pure gold going out, three to a side, like a face, with a seventh singular central trunk, reminding us of the importance of the mouth and the other gates of the face.

How did the Creator create this world?

Was it with a magic wand? Was it with a snap of the Divine finger? No. It was with words!

"And the Creator – *said* – let there be light, and there was light."[12]

We too create worlds with our words.

If we speak violently we create a little world of violence and conflict for ourselves and those around us. And when we speak words of love and affection, that then becomes the world in which we live.

We are told in the Torah to love the other as we would wish to be loved. Sometimes people get very good at speaking kindly and intimately to others while reserving a nasty brutal inner voice for themselves. This is not kosher. We create inner worlds with our inner words. Kind people will often tell themselves "you are no good," "you are going to fail," "people don't like you" … People will say things to themselves that they would never say to another person. This is *Leshon Hara*! You need your inner voice to be your best friend! Pirke Avot teaches (2:18): "Do not be evil in your own eyes."

For an outwardly kind person we might say, "Do unto yourself as you would do to another." Speak to yourself with that same sweetness with which you would speak to a friend or a child. Actually, be even kinder.

A Voice Inside My Head
Rabbi Pesach Dahvid Stadlin

There's a voice inside my head that sometimes gets nasty and fresh. It has said things to me that I would never say to anyone

---

12   Genesis 1:3.

Part One

else. "You have failed at this before, you will fail at this again" ... "You are ugly" ... "You are not good enough."

Here's how I tricked that voice in my head:

Once when he was blabbering in my mind about how I was weak and unsure of everything in my life, I gave the voice a challenge. I said to this inner voice, "If you are truth, then I'll give you the microphone and you can speak out of my mouth for the next few minutes." Secretly, I know that my mouth is trained to speak only lovingly, in ways that promote healing, and it is guarded from speaking words of destruction. When the voice of self-deprecation that had been on a tirade in my mind tried to speak out loud, my mouth wouldn't let it through. It's a gate, and it wouldn't let the vile words through.

And I smiled.

The nasty voice in my mind became embarrassed and the wind quickly left its sails. The curse turned into a blessing as I asked my inner voice out loud to be more of an ally to me and support me. Things haven't been the same since. Any time a nasty voice starts rearing its ugly head, I just glance at my mouth, and it blushes.

A Prayer
Rabbi Elimelekh of Lizhensk

Almighty God, place in our hearts
The ability to see in every human being

Only positive attributes and not their faults,

And may everyone guide each other
On the path of righteousness
That is desirable in Your eyes,

And may there never arise
In our hearts hatred for anyone, Heaven forbid.

Amen, may it be Your will.

Words Can Kill
Anonymous

The dangers of bullying

It's hard to believe, but some nasty people think they're having fun when they tell kids online, kids they do not even know, that they should kill themselves.

In Great Britain and elsewhere, several young women could not stand the pressure, and, sadly, ended their lives.

These nasty people did not realize that words can kill.

One courageous young woman wanted to put a stop to this bullying online. She said: "I've been bullied on an anonymous website, and have been told to kill myself many times. It's easy for people to hide behind anonymity and bully, and it needs to be stopped."

Another person, equally angry about internet bullying, wrote: "When does the freedom of the internet become a cancer that destroys lives? Websites like this need to be taken down immediately. The governments need to get serious about the cyber-bullying issues across the globe. RIP."

Others joined the movement to end such murderous bullying. One said: "We also cannot forget that thousands of young people, as in the tragic case of Hannah Smith [a teenager who committed suicide], face a daily barrage of online abuse, death threats and harassment.

"Although they may not be in the public eye or have celebrity status, it's shocking that one in three young people are cyber-bullied, and one in 13 face persistent abuse online.

"We cannot stand by while innocent children lose their lives. Adults need to set an example for young people and we all have a responsibility to tackle this type of behavior and keep our children safe.

"We want internet service providers, schools, government and the police to come together and produce an anti-bullying strategy, to prove that this kind of behavior will not be tolerated.

"We urge any young person worried about cyber-bullying to visit BeatBullying.org for advice and support."

Part One

Say A Nice Thing
Rabbi Ari Enkin

The most prominent transgression that caused a person to become a *metzora* was the sin of forbidden speech. Forbidden speech, known as *Leshon Hara*, in Hebrew, refers to slander, gossip, tale-bearing, and other types of malicious talk that one should never say.

One who required atonement in Temple times for having spoken *Leshon Hara* was required to bring two birds as a sacrifice.

Why two birds?

One of the reasons given is that one bird was to atone for the sin of forbidden speech while one bird was "to atone for the sin of good speech."

Huh? A bird sacrifice was needed to atone for "the sin of good speech?" A sin? What's wrong with good speech? What's going on over here?

It is explained that "the sin of good speech" refers to nice things you could have said to someone, but didn't. You could have said "good morning," "hello," "how are you," "can I help you?" but you didn't. This is the "sin" of good speech: missing the opportunity to say something nice to someone. Missing the opportunity to help someone feel good and to have a better day.

We are told that one of the things that got Joseph out of jail back in Egypt was that he always had a nice thing to say to others. He was always offering a helping hand and an encouraging word. Because of this, he was always remembered favorably by all, which caused him to be summoned to interpret Pharaoh's dreams and ultimately led him to be freed.

This is probably the most important message from this week's Torah portion. Never miss an opportunity to say a nice thing to another person. Remember Joseph. You never know what saying a nice word to someone else might lead to.

Changing For The Better
Rabbi Dov Peretz Elkins and Rabbi Chaim Listfield

Judaism basically looks upon human nature in a positive vein, unlike other religious traditions which see humans as having been created inherently evil.

Yet, Judaism is not pollyanish. It recognizes what it calls our *Yetzer Hara*, our proclivity to do evil; our tendency to be selfish and neurotic. The aim is by performing *mitzvot* and studying Torah, to help our *Yetzer Hatov*, our good impulse, win over the *Yetzer Hara* in the battle for our soul.

Many writers have recognized our dual nature. Dostoevsky, writing in his novel *A Raw Youth*, describes the human being's "faculty of cherishing in his soul the loftiest ideal side by side with his greatest baseness, and all quite sincerely."

Likewise, the prominent psychiatrist and best-selling author, M. Scott Peck, in his book, *The Road Less Traveled*, that "We all have a healthy self and a sick self."

Rabbi Hayim Vital, sixteenth century author on Jewish ethics, wrote that in addition to God having implanted within us a good impulse, God also placed the *Yetzer Hara*, but that the *Yetzer Hara* is encased in a shell, and it's extremely difficult to reach it.

This is our human dilemma. To change for the better from our worst parts to our best; from our *Yetzer Hara* to our *Yetzer Hatov*.

It's easier to accomplish this formidable task when we recognize its difficulty. Thus, we include in the *Al Chet* litany the prayer for forgiveness for the times when our worst part got the better of us.

No Wrong Time to Say the Right Thing
Steve Goodier
www.lifesupportsystem.com

A cartoon depicts a woman shaking hands with her clergyman as she leaves. The caption says, "Thank you for the sermon. It was like water to a drowning man." Some compliments are better left unsaid.

Isn't it true that words carry with them immense power? Power to build up and power to tear down. Such was the case with the words of Mandy (not her real name), a woman who learned that there is no wrong time to say the right thing.

Part One

It was a cold, rainy day in March. Across the room in the retail store where Mandy worked, sat Laura, a woman about Mandy's age. Other workers did not like Laura; they thought of her as snobbish and aloof. And Mandy agreed.

But sweeping the bias from her eyes, she made up her mind to say something kind to Laura. Finally, she managed, "Do you know, Laura, that I've worked in this room with you for several years. And whenever I glance up I see your head silhouetted against the window there behind you. I think you have the prettiest profile and hair that I have ever seen on anybody." Her words were not insincere flattery. She meant it.

Laura looked up and began to cry. "That's the first kind word anybody has ever said to me in all the time I've worked here," she said.

Mandy discovered that Laura's aloofness was not due to snobbishness, but shyness. The two became friends. Other workers soon began to include Laura in their activities, and she blossomed like a flower that, for the first time, found sunlight. The right words, spoken in kindness, made all the difference.

Words carry the potential to tear down or to build up. But when they are both sincere and kind, they are instruments that wield great power. Never underestimate the potential and power of your words.

There is no wrong time to say the right thing. And there is no better time than now.

Leshon Hara and Leshon Hatov – Positive Speech
Rabbi Yechiel Eckstein

The priest shall order that two live clean birds and some cedar wood, scarlet yarn and hyssop be brought for the person to be cleansed.

Leviticus 14:4

In *Parshat Metzora*, we learn about the purification process for the individual who had been afflicted with a defiling skin disease. One of the stages involved bringing two birds to the priest. One bird was to be slaughtered, and the other bird was part of a ritual and ultimately set free. The Jewish sages explain that birds were specifically chosen for this purification ritual because they are creatures that constantly chirp and chatter. According to Jewish tradition, the sin of the afflicted person is inappropriate speech and so the birds were seen as fitting symbols for the sin at hand.

While this explanation makes sense, there are still two questions that can't be ignored. First, why use two birds? Second, if we are symbolically getting rid of inappropriate chatter, why set the second bird free?

The sages explain that if the process involved only one bird that was sacrificed, we may mistakenly think that *all* chatter and speech should be banished from our lives. The second bird teaches us that speech is not the problem. In fact, our ability to speak is one of our greatest virtues! It's how we use our words that matters. The bird that was sacrificed represented bad speech. The second bird symbolized all the wonderful things that can be done with our words. That bird was set free to chatter away happily.

Consider these 10 ways that we can use the power of speech for good:

- Pray. Praise God, thank Him, and ask for your needs.
- Share God's Word with family, friends, and neighbors.
- Say "I love you," or let someone know you care.
- Say "I'm sorry," or give someone the gift of forgiveness.
- Say "Thank you!" as often as you can.
- Say a blessing – on the food you eat or to the people you meet.
- Say "Amen!" This one word gives more power to all other words.
- Ask someone, "How are you?" and mean it.
- Give someone encouragement. It may make all the difference in their world.
- Give someone a compliment. It may just change their day.
- If we focus on the great things that we can say – and should say – every day, we'll be so busy saying positive words that we won't even have time for gossip or other negative words.

With prayers for *shalom*, peace.

Part One

Leshon Hatov – Healing with Words
Rabbi Yechiel Eckstein

A woman once shared a powerful story about how kind words can have a huge impact on our lives. One night, her father arrived home from work and sat down at the table for dinner. After a long and stressful day, the only "dinner" his wife had managed to make was two pieces of extremely burnt toast and a jar of jam.

The woman, then just a child, remembers that evening as she sat waiting to see if her father would notice and comment on the charred bread. Instead, he ate the toast and began asking her about her day. She doesn't recall her answer, but she remembers that it was then her mother apologized for the burnt toast. Her father's response? "Honey, I love burnt toast!"

Later that night, at bedtime, she asked her father if he really did love burnt toast. He took her in his arms and said, "Your mom had a long and tough day, and she was really tired. Burnt toast doesn't hurt anyone, but words do."

That father was a hero that night. He saved his wife, his daughter, and himself from what could have been a catastrophic evening for them all.

What might have happened if he had made his wife feel badly? What if he had gotten angry? What if he simply stated that he hated burnt toast for dinner? All those responses would have been extremely hurtful. Instead, the man chose kindness and used his words to strengthen his wife and encourage her.

In Proverbs we read: *"Gracious words are a honeycomb, sweet to the soul and healing to the bones."* Long before modern medicine officially recognized the mind-body connection, King Solomon taught us that when we soothe the soul with kind words, it will have a positive impact on the body as well. When we speak with love and kindness, we bring healing to the body and soul.

It's no accident that the Hebrew word for "speaking," *daber,* is connected to the word *davar,* meaning "thing." This is because once our words leave our mouths, they ultimately become something tangible – either for bad or for good.

It's so easy to forget ourselves and to speak harshly as a gut reaction to something upsetting someone may have said or done to us. But let us learn from this lesson how we can turn everything around for the better and how we, too, can be the hero in someone's life by simply speaking kind and encouraging words to them.

If we pause before we speak and consider the impact our words might have, we can choose to take the better course – to soothe, to heal, and to love. With prayers for *shalom*, peace.

Positive Words
Rabbi Yisroel Jungreis

Parshas Behar contrasts monetary abuse, *Onoas Mamon,* vs verbal abuse, *Onoas Divorim*. The Talmud says verbal abuse is more severe because we are unable to estimate the pain it causes while monetary abuse can be estimated to the exact penny. Money can be paid back, but words cannot be taken back.

In the book of *mitzvos*, "*Sefer Hachinuch*", it says how careful we have to be with harsh words directed at children. Verbal abuse also includes certain nicknames that can hurt a child's feelings. The Talmud in Bava Metzi'a says a man should be very careful regarding verbally abusing his wife since a woman's tears come easily. Rabbi Shimon Bar Yochai says after the Temple was destroyed the gates of prayer have been sealed but the gate of tears caused by verbal abuse remains open. A man must be careful with his wife's honor because blessing is only found in one's home, because of his wife.

Shlomo HaMelech, King Solomon, said, "*Chaim Biyad Haloshon* – life is in the hands of the tongue." Just a simple good morning and asking how are you doing especially during these challenging times can work wonders to lift a person's spirit. I remember coming home from school when I was nine years old and my mother the Rebbitzen would be teaching a Torah class in the kitchen, she said to me, "Yisroel, say hello to everyone." I will never forget that message. We need to instruct children to always say good morning and thank you to the doorman, bus drivers or anyone who is helping them.

The Talmud says better to give the white of your smile than the

Part One

white of a glass of milk. A glass of milk is a temporary enjoyment but the effect of a beautiful smile remains forever. When we go to a store or bank we should put away our cellphones, when we are speaking to the teller or when we are checking out. It's called *derech eretz*, the proper thing to do.

A few years ago the Rabbi at the Empire poultry plant accidentally locked himself in the deep freezer. The security guard who found him said I knew the Rabbi was still here because he always greets me with a good morning and he would never leave without saying good night. When I saw the Rabbi this morning I knew he was still here because I did not receive my traditional "have a wonderful evening, Bob." May HaShem always give us the ability to share good news with each other.

Speech In The Positive

One-fourth of all the *Al Chet* litany in the Yom Kippur service is made up of sins of the tongue. Here are some thoughts which remind us how to make positive speech a priority in the coming year.

The Talmud equates speaking *Leshon Hara* with flagrant atheism, with adultery, and with murder. In fact, it is worse than murder since it simultaneously destroys three people: the one who relates the gossip, the one who listens to it, and the one it concerns.

Part Two
Leshon Hara – Negative Speech

Part Two

Permissible Leshon Hara
Rabbi Yisroel Jungreis

"*Lo Saylaich Rochil Biamecha*" do not be a talebearer amongst your people. "*Lo Samod al Dam Rayecha*" do not stand idly by the blood of your neighbor (Kedoshim 19-16). Rashi defines a talebearer as a person who enjoys inciting strife and relating *Leshon Hara*, like a person who goes from house to house to spy out and find gossip in order reveal it in the public market place. Do not stand by the blood of your people means you are required to warn a person of potential danger that might be coming in their direction. Rabbi Moshe Sternbach gives us a reason why these laws are in the same sentence. A person must always refrain from *Leshon Hara*, gossip, and slander but there are times a person is obligated to reveal information. This is called *Leshon Hara Toeles* – required and constructive information. If you know for instance a person is getting involved in a business or personal relationship that might be detrimental or dangerous to their wellbeing you must reveal the information and not stand idly by. By not revealing, you will be standing by the blood of your fellow Jew. The Chofetz Chaim gives three rules before one can reveal *Leshon Hara* which is *Toeles* – for constructive purposes:

1- The speaker must be certain that the information is accurate.
2- The speaker should not be exaggerating.
3- The speaker has no personal interests in seeing the shiduch or partnership being rejected or dissolved.

May the holy Chofetz Chaim's blessing of speaking positive speech always be guiding us with blessing and salvation.

Biblical Speech
Rabbi Aryeh Citron[1]

When Miriam spoke negatively about her brother, Moses, she was rebuked by God and afflicted with the skin disease of *tzaraat*

---

1 www.chabad.org.

Leshon Hara – Negative Speech

as a punishment. Due to Moses' prayers, she was cured soon after, but still needed to remain outside of the camp for seven days.[2] Aaron, who had listened to her negative speech without protesting, was also punished, but not as severely.[3]

Unfortunately, the spies who were sent soon afterwards to Israel did not take a lesson from this story, and they too spoke negatively about the Land of Israel. The result was that the Israelites of that generation all died in the desert.

The idolatrous armies of King Ahab were successful in their battles, because they did not have the sin of *Leshon Hara*. In fact, we find that *Leshon Hara*, negative talk, is a sin that has caused numerous tragedies for the Jewish people, and indeed the world, since the very beginning of history.

Some examples of this are:

- The Midrash tells us that the snake slandered God to Eve when convincing her to eat of the Tree of Knowledge.[4]
- Joseph spoke negatively to his father, Jacob, about his brothers, causing them to hate him. This led to their selling him, and ultimately caused the Egyptian exile.[5]
- At first Moses wondered why the Jews deserved their difficult slavery in Egypt. When he heard that there were talebearers amongst them, he said that he then understood why they deserved this fate.[6]
- The slander of Doeg, King Saul's chief shepherd and the head of the Sanhedrin, caused the massacre of nearly an entire city of *kohanim*.[7] In fact, the armies of King Saul lost their battles with the Philistines as a result of the slander that people spoke against (then future) King David.[8] (On the other hand, the armies of the notorious King Ahab were successful in their battles, despite the

---

2 See Numbers, ch. 12. The commentaries to vv. 1-2 discuss what it was that she said.
3 See Rashi to verse 9, and Rabbeinu Bechayei to verse 1.
4 See Bereishit Rabbah 19:4 for the snake's slanderous claim.
5 See Genesis, ch. 37, and Bereishit Rabbah 84:7.
6 See Exodus 2:14 and Rashi on this verse.
7 See I Samuel 22:9ff.
8 Midrash Shocher Tov 7:8.

Part Two

fact that they were idolatrous, because they did not have the sin of *Leshon Hara*.⁽⁹⁾)

- According to the Talmud, it was the slander of Jews by Jews that actually brought about the destruction of the Second Temple.⁽¹⁰⁾

The laws of *Leshon Hara* are too lengthy to include in one article. In fact, Rabbi Israel Meir Kagan Hakohen of Radin wrote an entire book about these laws. The book is called *Chofetz Chaim,* which caused the author to be known as the "Chofetz Chaim" too. The name is inspired by the verse in Psalms, "Whoever of you desires life *(chofetz chaim)* ... guard your tongue from evil."⁽¹¹⁾

Nevertheless, here is a brief overview of some of the laws, mostly gleaned from *Chofetz Chaim*:

1. *Leshon Hara* literally means "bad talk." This means that it is forbidden to speak negatively about someone else, even if it is true.⁽¹²⁾

2. It is also forbidden to repeat anything about another, even if it is not a negative thing. This is called *rechilut*.⁽¹³⁾

3. It is also forbidden to listen to *Leshon Hara*. One should either reprimand the speaker, or, if that is not possible, one should extricate oneself from that situation.⁽¹⁴⁾

4. Even if one has already heard the *Leshon Hara*, it is forbidden to believe it. On the contrary, one should always judge one's fellow favorably.⁽¹⁵⁾

5. If one has already heard the *Leshon Hara*, he is forbidden to believe it. Nevertheless, one may suspect that the *Leshon Hara* is true, and take the necessary precautions

---

9 Ibid.
10 Talmud, Gittin 55b-56a.
11 Psalms 34:12-13.
12 See Shulchan Aruch Harav, Orach Chaim 156:10.
13 See Leviticus 19:16, and Mishneh Torah, Hilchot De'ot, chapter 7.
14 Chofetz Chaim 6:2, based on Talmud, Ketubot 5a and other sources.
15 Ibid. Based on Talmud, Pesachim 118a, and commentary of Rashbam ibid. s.v. Hamekabel.

Leshon Hara – Negative Speech

to protect oneself.⁽¹⁶⁾

6. It is forbidden to even make a motion that is derogatory towards someone.⁽¹⁷⁾

7. One may not even retell a negative event without using names, if the listeners might be able to figure out who is being spoken of.⁽¹⁸⁾

8. In certain circumstances, such as to protect someone from harm, it is permissible or even obligatory to share negative information. As there are many details to this law, one should consult a competent Rabbi to learn what may be shared in any particular situation.⁽¹⁹⁾

9. Learn more: Whistle-Blowing in Jewish Law.

Signs

Great minds discuss ideas.
Average minds discuss events.
Small minds discuss people.
Sign in a pizza shop, Miami Beach, FL

This Phone May Not Be Used For Gossip!
Sign above the telephone
in the home of a pious Hasid in Borough Park

---

16   Talmud, Niddah 61a. See Jeremiah, ch. 41, where the story is told of how Gedaliah did not believe *Leshon Hara* at all, and thus allowed his adversaries into his palace. They eventually killed him, as well as most of his men.

17   In the words of King Solomon: "An unscrupulous man, a man of violence, he walks with a crooked mouth; he winks with his eyes, shuffles with his feet, points with his fingers. Contrariness is in his heart; he plots evil at all times; he incites quarrels" (Proverbs 6:12-15).

18   Chofetz Chaim 3:4.

19   See Chofetz Chaim, ch.10.

Part Two

The Iron Dome Against Leshon Hara
Rabbi Jonny Sack

After *Parshat Yitro's* revelation of Hashem to the entire Jewish nation at Mt. Sinai and the giving of the Torah, this week, in *Parshat Mishpatim*, the Torah brings that spirituality down to earth with the teaching of tangible worldly *mitzvot*: everything from not taking a bribe to not cooking meat and milk together.

There is one particular *Lo Taaseh* taught in this week's *parsha* which presents a particularly difficult challenge to many and despite being one of the most serious of sins, many are unaware of it or how to work on preventing themselves from its transgression. This *avera* comes up on a daily basis and holds extremely severe negative ramifications, having the ability to completely undermine our growth as a person. This is the mitzvah of *"Lo Tisa Shema Shav."* This is the source of the Torah prohibition to not believe or even listen[20] to *Leshon Hara*.[21] The literal translation is "Do not bear (carry) a false hearing" or in easier language *"Don't carry in your heart the negative things you may hear about others."*

Most Jews today are well aware of the damage and seriousness of speaking *Leshon Hara* which constitutes negative comments about other people, even if they are true. The Talmud teaches that *Leshon Hara* is parallel in severity to Murder, Idolatry and Immoral relationships – combined! Another statement in the Talmud teaches that Hashem cannot "co-exist" with one who speaks *Leshon Hara*. Midrashim liken *Leshon Hara* to an arrow which, unlike a sword, strikes from afar without the victim's knowledge or expectation and once "shot" can never be retracted. Today, with Facebook and the like it takes only a slight movement of the finger or a click to spread *Leshon Hara* to thousands of people instantaneously, "killing" the victim's reputation, self-esteem, career, friendships, relationships ... the list goes on.

This applies to the one who is speaking/writing *Leshon Hara*. What about the one who listens in, reads or who believes what is said or who passively sits in on a conversation where someone else is the one doing the talking? Is that really so bad? The Chofetz

---

20 Chofetz Chaim, Hil. *Leshon Hara*, Clal 6, siif 2 and see the Beer Mayim Chaim there for the sources.

21 See Chofetz Chaim Peticha, and Hilchot *Leshon Hara* Clal 6. Mechilta, *Parshat Mishpatim*. See Rambam hil. Deot Perek 7.

Leshon Hara – Negative Speech

Chaim quotes the Rambam who mentions that believing *Leshon Hara* is actually worse in some respects than speaking it![22]

Imagine the following situation, you are sitting with some friends and chatting about things and someone in the group begins to say something along the lines of: "Once you get to know Bob, you realize how irritating he can actually be." What do you do? It is one thing to work on your own speech and try to slowly learn how to stay far away from saying anything negative about people, but to control another person's speech is seemingly impossible. What are we supposed to do in situations like this? Have we transgressed this serious prohibition, even against our will?

Let's delve into this practical halachic area and discover something both profound, thought provoking and instructive for how we conduct our conversations with others.

Firstly, we need to understand the damage that hearing/believing *Leshon Hara* can cause. Spiritually speaking, Chazal explain that our experience in the next world and for eternity is based purely on how we behave in this world. The book *Shaarei Kedusha* by Rav Chaim Vital (ztz'l) explains how our soul is made up of spiritual limbs and sinews that parallel our body. When we do *mitzvot* in this world with our body we bring spiritual life-charge, like a battery, to the corresponding soul parts that we did the mitzvah with. When we sin, we attach impurity to the corresponding soul part. Listening to *Leshon Hara* damages the spiritual ear of the soul so to speak, and believing *Leshon Hara* as true, brings impurity to the soul's heart.[23]

On a "this-worldly" plane, the damage is also profound. The language in the Torah is very instructive. When it teaches us not to listen and believe *Leshon Hara* it actually uses the phrase *"do not carry."* Why *carry*? Because when you hear something negative about someone else and you let it sink into your memory bank, you carry it around with you. You may have heard something negative about someone years ago, but every time you see that person the first thing that unavoidably pops into your head is a little voice reminding you of the negative trait you once heard. Worse still, you may begin to project that negative information you heard about them onto their current actions so that the slightest

---

22 Rambam Hil. Deot 7:3, Chofetz Chaim, clal 6, siif 1.
23 See the introduction to *Shmirat Halashon* by the Chofetz Chaim where he explains this in detail.

Part Two

resemblance they might show to the *Leshon Hara* you heard about them becomes a concrete reminder for you that what you heard was true.

Let's say you heard that a certain wealthy acquaintance is miserly with his money. When you interact with him you will notice the slightest resemblance to miserliness and the voice goes off in your head *"they were so right about him."* It is as if we paint pictures of how we will judge others based on the various reports we have heard about them. Then we carry these frames around with us and each time we see the people we squash them into the negative frame.

From a relationship perspective, believing *Leshon Hara* can lead to major hurt and fighting. In moments of frustration or anger with a friend or family member we can let loose of negative things that we heard and have been carrying around about others and cause untold damage to relationships with those we love saying something like, "Well now I see what so and so meant when they said you were so (insert negative comment here)!"

Listening in on or reading *Leshon Hara* also trains us to enjoy the belittling of others. There are magazines, websites and TV shows out there that draw thousands of viewers or readers purely lured by the excitement of hearing the latest "goss." People who speak/write *Leshon Hara*, often do so because they enjoy the sensation of pulling someone else down. It makes them feel better about themselves. We must remind ourselves of the famous line – "those you can't be great, be-little." Comments like *"He is not as nice as you think, he actually has a real ugly side to him"* or *"She might be beautiful on the outside but she is so full of herself"* or posts on Facebook that draw attention to people doing embarrassing things which they regret, are often said/written by people who are jealous or feel some lacking in themselves which they try and fill through taking bites out of other people. When we enjoy hearing/reading these things we are giving the speaker our tick of approval and sinking into the same psychological trap that feeds our ego off others shortcomings.

The important point to remember is that with *Leshon Hara*, the listener is the one in control of whether the evil gets off the ground or not. If you are talking to someone and they belittle someone else, they are passing you a package of negativity to carry and you can simply say "No." If you do that, then as bad as the speaker is,

Leshon Hara – Negative Speech

you have stopped the negativity from having its impact. You have knocked the missile off its course mid-flight – Iron Dome style.

How do you do this?

There are a number of practical *halachot* here to keep in mind: Firstly, in general, the more of an expert you are at judging people favorably, the less you will believe *Leshon Hara*. In addition, the more you show the people you socialize with that you don't like hearing *Leshon Hara*, the more careful they will be from speaking it. One would also need to ask him/herself – am I spending time with people who build others or try to destroy them? Socializing with habitual *Leshon Hara* speakers is something that Chazal severely warned against, saying that when the group is inscribed above, all who are present are inscribed as part of a *Chavurat Resha* (an evil grouping), even if you are absolutely passive.[24]

If you already have close friends or family members who speak *Leshon Hara* often, you would be wise to gently approach the subject with them. A subtle and successful way to do this is to present the issue as something that you are personally trying to work on and ask them for their help in the matter. If done correctly, they should not feel judged by you but rather feel that you are asking their wise counsel and practical assistance in your own personal mission. The result will hopefully be a heightened sensitivity to *Shmirat Halashon* in your future conversations.

More specifically, what do you do in a situation where you hear *Leshon Hara*? (We will just raise some of the basic concepts here as they appear in the Chofetz Chaim. This is not meant to serve as a final halachic guide.)

If you are speaking to a friend and they begin to speak *Leshon Hara*, you should ideally try and change the subject. To do this you could excitedly interrupt with some news that changes the subject; "Wait! I have to tell you something! I (insert some random news that will steer the conversation in a different direction). If this will not work, then you need to think to yourself: will this friend listen to me if I gently say I would rather not hear such things? If the person will listen, or even if you are not sure about it, you have an obligation to stop your friend from saying the *Leshon Hara*.[25] You

---

24 See Chofetz Chaim, Hil, *Leshon Hara*, Clal 6, Siif 5 and 6. This could also involve a *bitul* of a positive commandment of "*boh tidbak*" and other Torah *mitzvot*. See Clal 6, Beer Mayim Chayim 17 and the *petichah* to the sefer.

25 This is a mitzvah of Tochacha and is brought in the Chofetz Chaim

Part Two

must be very gentle and sensitive in doing so. You could just say "Can we please speak about something else" or "wait, let's think of a different topic to chat about." Just be clear so they get the picture, but gentle so you don't hurt them in the process. If they are someone who you know won't stop so easily and will speak further negativity as a result of your attempt to stop them, then rebuke is forbidden and the best thing to do is leave the conversation. Go to the bathroom, make a phone call, do something to get out of the situation. If this is not an option, then you have no choice but to be strong. You can drift off mentally as they are talking (some people are good at this in non-*Leshon Hara* situations anyway) but at least *do not believe* what is being said, *don't enjoy* what is being said and *do not show your agreement* with what is being said.[26]

When you are in a group, again try and change the subject if you can. It is often much harder to stop the *Leshon Hara* in these situations because the speaker will often be embarrassed by you implying that they did something wrong, and in an effort to not be discredited, they might shift the attack onto you with something like *"Oh, you are such a Tzadeket? As if you don't speak about people too!"* or worse. In such a case, you should ideally just get up and leave. This is a subtle way of teaching everyone sensitivity to *Leshon Hara* and showing them that you don't want to be a part of such talk (it is a big mitzvah to do so). If leaving is not an option, then try and fill your mind to think of something else. If you can't avoid hearing, then once again, as above, put on your battle gear and fight with your *Yetzer Hara* to *not believe, not enjoy* and *not show you agree* with what you are hearing. To do this, tell yourself that what is being said is not true and the speaker is just exaggerating, making it up or got the story wrong. Remind yourself of all those stories you have heard about misjudging people, and judge the person you are hearing about positively. If you can do that, and block your heart from letting in the *Leshon Hara*, then you have done an enormous mitzvah.[27]

---

numerous times. See Hil. *Leshon Hara*, clal 6, siif 5 and the Beer Mayim Chaim there in the name of Rabeinu Yona.

26   Ibid, siif 5.

27   Again, this is not meant to serve as a final halachic guide. At times it is best to verbalize a positive way of looking at the story in front of the group to reverse the negativity of what has been said. At other times this is not advisable. It depends on the speaker of the *Leshon Hara* and his/her personality. There

Finally, there will of course be times when you need to hear something negative about someone else for a constructive purpose, for example to save yourself from harm they might cause you or others. The details of when and how this is allowed requires more explanation and I urge you to study these *halachot* in detail as they appear in the Chofetz Chaim, Clal 6.

In the meantime, may we take these messages and internalize them to become hyper-sensitive to what we let enter our ears and hearts and promote positive speech and kind words wherever we are.

Avoiding Leshon Hara – Messages
Rabbi Pinchas Peli

- For lack of wood, fire is extinguished, Without a talebearer, strife is stilled. (Proverbs 26:20)

Message: Unless gossip is "fueled", it dies down and is forgotten.

- The gossiper stands in Syria and kills in Rome. (Yerushalmi, Peah 1:1)

Message: Gossip's reach and power are far and wide.

- Your friend has a friend, and your friend's friend has a friend, so be cautious in your speech. (Anonymous)

Message: Gossip spreads quickly. You tell one "trustworthy" person, and that "trustworthy" person tells his/her "trustworthy" person, and before you know it ...

- A person who honors the tongue and uses it to speak words of Torah and *mitzvot* will be rewarded, but one who speaks slander and gossip brings much sorrow to the world. (*Tzenah Ure'ena* on Lev. 14:1-2)

are many more *halachot* that surface here and one is advised to learn clal 6 of Chofetz Chaim in detail to become familiar with the various intricacies of these laws.

Part Two

Message: A good strategy for overcoming the tendency to gossip is to be preoccupied with positive words, such as Torah and *mitzvot*.

- One may discount the value of words. After all, they can be neither seen nor touched. However, so it is with the wind, which can be neither seen nor touched. Yet it is capable of destroying entire worlds. (Anonymous)

Message: It is a common tendency, and easy to underestimate the potential damage of speech. Yet we must not, for its power for destruction is beyond our wildest imagination.

- There is hardly a day when we are spared from *Leshon Hara*. (Baba Batra 164b)

Message: Gossip and slander are ubiquitous and pernicious; beware of speaking or listening to them.

Just Talkin'
Rabbi Jack Riemer[28] – A Letter to Dear Abby

Dear Abby: When I was growing up, my mother and the other ladies in her friendship group were very polite to each other. However, when one of them was not present, the others would talk about the absent one. They would compliment a woman to her face, and then criticize her as soon as she walked away.

Mother always defended this behavior as a "harmless" pastime. I don't know if it hurt the people who were the butt of gossip or not, but I do know how harmful it was to me, and to the other children who were listening.

Their behavior taught me not to trust anyone, especially those people who were nice to my face. Instead, I trusted abusive people, because I thought they were being honest. I ended up running with a bad crowd and found myself dating abusive men because I felt that I couldn't trust polite guys.

When someone complimented me, I didn't believe it, so I never

---

28   Rabbi Riemer is the author of *Finding God in Unexpected Places* and *The Day I Met Father Isaac in the Supermarket*.

developed self-confidence. I was afraid people were laughing at me behind my back. I had trouble making friends with other girls because I was afraid to open up and reveal my feelings, for fear that whatever I said would become grist for gossip.

After a year of therapy, I have finally found the self-confidence that I lacked. My sisters have not been so fortunate. Neither has any close friends, and both are married to abusive men.

Abby, please inform your readers that there is nothing "harmless" about gossip, especially to the children who are listening.

Signed: Hoping to Gain the Ability to Trust, in Georgia

Abby answered that letter by sending this woman and her readers a copy of a vignette that she had published before. The author is unknown. Who knows why? Perhaps out of modesty or perhaps because the author was afraid that she would be maligned for having written it? Whatever, this is the vignette.

I Am Nobody's Friend

My name is Gossip. I have no respect for justice.
I maim without killing. I break hearts and ruin lives.
I am cunning and malicious, and I improve with age.
The more I am quoted, the more I am believed.

My victims are helpless. They cannot protect themselves against me because they do not know my name or face.

To track me down is impossible. The harder you try, the more elusive I become.

I am nobody's friend. Believe me, I am nobody's friend, not even those who traffic in me.

Once I tarnish a reputation, it is never the same.
I can destroy careers and I can wreck marriages.
I cause sleepless nights, heartaches, and distrust.
I make innocent people cry into their pillows.

Even my name hisses. I am called gossip. I make headlines and headaches.

And then Abby added: Readers, before you repeat a story, ask yourselves: Is it true? Is it harmless? Is it necessary? If it isn't, don't repeat it.

Part Two

Like An Arrow
Rabbi Bradley Artson

In the words of the Rabbis, "A loose tongue is like an arrow. Once it is shot, there is no holding it back." The Midrash notes that five times, the word "Torah," teaching, is used to refer to *tzaraat*. From this superfluous repetition, the sages derive that "one who utters evil reports is considered in violation of the entire five books of the Torah."

A marvelous tale is told of a wandering merchant who came into a town square, offering to sell the elixir of life. Of course, large crowds would surround him, each person eager to purchase eternal youth. When pressed, the merchant would bring out the Book of Psalms, and show them the verse "Who desires life? Keep your tongue from evil and your lips from guile."

In an age awash in corrosive mistrust, a lack of confidence in our public leaders, and an alienating sense of loneliness and isolation, there is little hope of establishing real community until we learn to speak a new language – one of responsibility, kindness and compassion.

Rather than spreading rumors to make others look bad, we can devise empathic explanations for why someone might have acted in a disappointing way.

Rather than repeating a racist joke, we can focus attention on the shared humanity of all people.

Rather than speaking about other people, we can speak to them, out of love and a desire to live in a shared community together.

By learning to channel and control our speech, we will transform our world from one of isolation and cynicism to one of community and trust. Isn't that what the rule of God is all about?

Words That Wound
Rabbi Joseph Telushkin

The most famous event in *Beha'alotkha* is the punishment God inflicts on Miriam, Moses' sister, for speaking ill of him with Aaron

Leshon Hara – Negative Speech

(Numbers 12:1ff.). God confronts Miriam and Aaron. God is furious with them for gossiping about Moses and as punishment makes Miriam's skin turn leprous. Aaron appeals to Moses, who directs a five-word prayer to God, "O God, pray heal her" and Miriam is immediately cured.

The Rabbis see in Miriam's sufferings a punishment for the grave sin of *Leshon Hara*, gossiping. Elsewhere, the Torah teaches, "Do not go about as a talebearer among your people" (Leviticus 19:16). The Rabbis understand this law as forbidding one from saying anything negative about another person, even if it is true, unless the listener has legitimate need of this information.

In the Talmud, the Rabbis compared gossip to murder (Arachin 15b), for it too is irrevocable. The impossibility of undoing damage done by harmful gossip is underscored in a Chasidic tale about a man who went through his community slandering the Rabbi. One day, feeling remorseful, he begged the Rabbi for forgiveness and said he was willing to do penance. The Rabbi told him to take several feather pillows, cut them open, and scatter the feathers to the winds. The man did so, but when he returned to tell the Rabbi that he had fulfilled his request, he was told, "Now go and gather all the feathers."

The man protested, "But that is impossible."

"Of course it is. And though you may sincerely regret the evil you have done and truly desire to correct it, it is as impossible to repair the damage done by your words as it will be to recover the feathers."

The Power To Speak
Rabbi Ephraim Rubinger

One of the aspects of our Jewish religious tradition which a lot of people really do not know about is that a great deal of time and energy is paid to the concept of *Shmirat Halashon*, "purity of speech." I know that the very sound of the term "purity of speech" seems anachronistic in these days of negative campaigning, of "anything goes" language on the TV and in the movies, and a culture which in general does not think that words are terribly important.

Part Two

However Judaism *does* think that words are important and that speech is important. In fact in Jewish tradition it is the capacity for speech that is the feature that most distinguishes human life from animal life. In the Targum Onkelos, the Aramaic translation of the Torah, the verse "God breathed into Adam the breath of life" is translated as, "God breathed into Adam the power to speak." "The breath of life" – of HUMAN life, is defined as the power of speech ... and that is a gift from God. If speech is a gift from God, then obviously it should be treasured and not cheapened through gossip or by using it to insult someone or through constant use of obscenities. Speech ought to be pure, ought to be holy.

Put Your Yetzer Hara In Its Place
Irving M. Bunim

Let us recall one of the statements of confession in the prayer of *Al Chet* that we recite on Yom Kippur, The Day of Atonement: "(Forgive us) for the sins we have committed before Thee through the evil inclination." This is surely a strange category of wrongdoing to include in a long list of sins. For this statement would seem to cover every conceivable kind of transgression.

Does man ever commit a sin without an evil inclination? Then shouldn't this one sentence make the rest of *Al Chet* superfluous?

The answer is that these words of confession refer not to our actual deeds of evil and wrong, but to a "bonus," an increment that we acquire with every transgression. For with every misdeed we build up and develop the *Yetzer Hara*, the passion for evil within ourselves. The very first time a person sins, he generally feels concerned and a bit frightened at the time. There are pangs of guilt. But after the sin is over and done with, the *Yetzer Hara* feels more securely entrenched. It has grown stronger, and is now quite a "big fellow." In a while it comes around, all confidence and smiles, and whispers, as it were, "See, it did not hurt at all And think of the pleasure and benefits you gained! We ought to do it again!" Soon the sin becomes the usual thing to do.

Yes, we have sinned before the Almighty through our *Yetzer Hara*. With every wrong deed, we gradually build the evil inclination into a Frankenstein monster that we permit to dominate us. If you can put your *Yetzer* in its place and keep it there, only then are you truly strong.

To Vex With Words
Rabbi Kassel Abelson

I recently passed a novelty shop where my eye was caught by a set of wind-up teeth, which chattered feverishly, producing the unedifying sound "yackety yack." Underneath was a sign saying "Words are cheap." The creator of the gadget was calling attention to the fact that words, unaccompanied by action, have little value. This idea also lies behind the contemptuous expression, "It's only words."

From the viewpoint of Judaism, words are not cheap. Quite the contrary, they are infinitely precious. Through words we maintain contact with each other. They are the bridge over which we move into each other's lives. Words unite and words can divide. Words can heal and words can wound. Words can lift us up or crush us. Words can bolster our confidence or rob us of our dignity.

Rashi, the famous commentator on the Torah, was moved to do something very unusual for him: taking a phrase out of context, he uses it as the basis for a stern warning on the power of words. "*V'lo tonu ish et amito* – Do not wrong one another, but fear your God: for I the Lord am your God" (Lev. 25: 17). In context the warning refers to fairness in real estate transactions. Rashi tells us, however, that the Torah is really concerned with something else: *Kan Hizhir Al Dna-at D'varim* – Here the Torah warns us against vexing others with words. *Dna-at D'varim* refers to hurting another person's feelings, irritating him, and getting him upset by what we say. It seems to me that the reason Rashi makes such a point of stressing the seriousness of *Dna-at D'varim* is because it is a particularly Jewish sin.

Several years ago I attended a pastoral counseling conference in which Rabbis and clergymen discussed questions that troubled the members of the group.

One clergyman asked us, "How would you counsel with a drunken father who beats his daughter and throws her down the stairs?"

Part Two

There were many attempts to answer this question. My honest answer was, "As a Rabbi, I have never had such a case." As I thought about it, I realized that in interpersonal relationships, Jews seldom resort to physical violence. Jewish children are sometimes spanked, but rarely do we hear of Jewish victims of child or spouse abuse. The reaction to these complaints is usually shock, for interpersonal violence among Jews, though it does exist, is not common.

This is not to say that there is no anger or aggression among Jews. There certainly is. But anger among Jews takes different forms. We attack and we beat with words. We wound, not with knives but with cutting remarks. Many of you may have seen the show "Who's afraid of Virginia Wolf". I've seen it on the stage, on the screen and several times in my study.

L'Haknit Bidvarim (to vex with words) is a widespread Jewish vice that should be avoided, because it does a great deal of damage. One of our sages in a play on words pointed out that the Hebrew word *L'Haknit* (to vex or irritate) has the same letters in it as *L'Haktin*, which means "to belittle." Vexing with words diminishes a person's sense of worth and dignity. As Rashi warns, this, too, is a serious wrong.

It has become fashionable to consider it a virtue to be open and honest. We are told that we should not conceal our feelings, nor harbor, anger, but rather that it is good to learn how to "tell it like it is."

Often when we "tell it like it is," we feel better. We have gotten our anger out. We may feel better, but how does the other person feel? In being honest about our feelings, did we consider the impact that our words had on the person to whom they were addressed? We wounded another's feelings so we can feel better. We enhanced our own sense of worth by belittling others and making them feel worthless.

Rashi, a thousand years ago, went far beyond where many distinguished psychologists stand today, warning us to be aware that poorly used words are both dangerous and destructive. He cautions us to be as careful not to belittle as we are not to beat. Further, he tells us that good interpersonal relationships involve not only being open and honest, but accepting responsibility for all that we say. Words, says a Yiddish proverb, should be weighed, not counted.

Leshon Hara – Negative Speech

God will judge us and hold us responsible for what we say and how we say it, and for the impact our words have on others. For words are not cheap. Words are precious. Words are powerful and should be used with care.

Even If True – Gossip Is Still A Sin
Rabbi Shlomo Riskin

Miriam and Aaron began speaking against Moses because of the dark-skinned woman he had married.
Numbers 12:1

In *Behalotcha,* we read of Miriam's loose tongue and God's quick punishment: "When the cloud left its place over the Tent, Miriam was leprous, white, as snow" (Numbers 12:10).

Who isn't aware that slander and libel are condemned. But try to tell a magazine specializing in gossip that parading the mistakes and sins of others is forbidden!

Maimonides, in his Laws of Knowledge, Ch. 7, Law 1, cites the verse: "You shall not be a talebearer among your people" (Lev. 19:16), pointing out that the second part of the verse: "You shall not stand upon the blood of your brother," proves that gossip can "destroy the world." He cites the example of Doeg the Edomite, who reported to King Saul that David, whom Saul saw as his competitor and nemesis, had been granted sanctuary in the priestly city of Nov. Doeg spoke the truth, but his tale resulted in the slaughter of 85 priests as well as every man woman, child and beast in the well-meaning but unfortunate city of Nov (I Samuel Ch. 22).

Maimonides distinguishes between three categories of gossip, each of which is Biblically condemned: *rechilut* (talebearing), which he interprets to refer to even innocuous, but unnecessary, information about a third party; *Leshon Hara* which is negative but true information; and *motzi shem ra,* which is negative and untrue.

Take, for example, the complimentary comment, "Bob's son just finished law school." If said to a man whose own son was thrown out of law school, the words could be as sharp as a knife in the heart. Our tradition tells us that the malady translated as "leprosy" is the punishment for slander, the crime and the punishment linked linguistically because the word for "leper" – *metzora* – and the word for slander *motzi shem ra* – share a common sound, as if one were the echo of the other.

In analyzing the text describing Miriam's sin, we learn a great deal about the Biblical attitude toward gossip. All that is revealed by the text is that something was said concerning the Kushite woman. Rashi (loc cit) quotes the Sifri, which brings down the words of R. Natan who explains that Miriam happened to be next to Moses' wife Tziporah when Moses was informed that two men in the camp, Eldad and Medad, had begun to prophesy. Commiserating with the wives of Eldad and Medad, Tziporah shared her fear that their husbands might leave them as her husband had left her. Tziporah sees the burden of prophecy as including the cessation of marital relations; her husband's dedication to God having severed his ties with his wife.

Armed with this bit of intimacy, Miriam pulls along Aaron, and the gossip about Moses gets rolling, though the text merely hints at what transpired. This is why Rashi fills us in with the missing pieces, including the idea that a "Kushite woman" is synonymous with "beauty." Hence, according to Rashi, the Kushite is Tziporah and Miriam broadcasts her sister-in-law's feelings, subtly adding that Moses has become estranged from a beautiful and good woman.

An alternative interpretation by Joseph ben Kaspi (1279-1340) understands the verse to be a literal reference to Moses having taken a second wife, a Kushite, and this is why Miriam and Aaron are gossiping.

Common to both readings is the fact that nowhere is there the remotest suggestion that Miriam and Aaron are spreading untruths. Whatever they said about Moses is fact: either he left Tziporah or he took a second wife – neither of which is Biblically forbidden – yet this talk leads to Miriam's flesh turning leprous, a terrible condition for a person earlier described as a prophetess.

The clue to Miriam's sin is found in her motive. In the following verse, we read that Miriam and Aaron go on to say: "Is it to Moses exclusively that God speaks? Doesn't He also speak to us?" (Numbers 12:2).

Now we understand what they're driving at. Miriam is jealous of her brother Moses. By first cutting her brother down to size, she may be able to prove that he's not the only prophet in the desert. Talking about Tziporah might have been utterly innocuous, but in this context blackening Moses' reputation was part of an attempt to whiten her own – another reason why a talebearer suffers a disease that make's one's skin as white as snow.

Rabbi Yisrael Salanter, founder of the Musar movement in the 19th century, illustrated the attraction of slander this way: If I want to appear bigger than someone, I can either climb a ladder and keep reaching for higher branches, or I can push my competitor into a pit so deep he'll never crawl out. The latter is the function of slander.

After the question, "doesn't He also speak to us?" God clarified the difference between the prophecies of Miriam and the prophecies of Moses: "If someone among you experiences Divine prophecy, then when I make Myself known to him in a vision, I will speak to him in a dream. This is not true with My servant Moses, who is like a trusted servant throughout My house. With him I speak face to face. How can you not be afraid to speak against My servant?" (Numbers 11:6-8).

In God's defense of Moses, there is no reference to the Kushite woman; that isn't the real issue. What is at stake is the positioning and the purpose of a seemingly innocent remark.

The laws of kosher food – what one may or may not put *in* one's mouth – have always been easier to keep than the laws of kosher talk – what one may or may not allow *out* of one's mouth. Perhaps this principle is one reason why Maimonides quotes the dictum of the sages that idol worship, incest and murder remove a person from this world and the next, and that *Leshon Hara* is equivalent to all three.

Avoiding gossip can thus be a matter of life and death for at least three people: the gossiper, the one who hears it, and the one the gossip is about.

For the Sin of Leshon Hara
Chofetz Chaim (Rabbi Yisrael Meir Kagan HaKohen)

Those who listen to slanderous gossip are just as guilty as the

Part Two

talebearers. Repeated use of the evil tongue is like a silk thread made strong by hundreds of strands. The foul sin of talebearing often results in a chain of transgressions.

Leprosy was regarded as a punishment for slander because the two resemble each other: they are both slightly noticeable at the outset, and then develop into a chronic, infectious disease.

Furthermore, the slanderer separates husband from wife, brother from brother, and friend from friend; he is therefore afflicted with the disease which separates him from society.

One sinful Jew can do harm to all his people, who are like a single body sensitive to the pain felt by any of its parts.

The Power of Words
Rabbi Seymour J. Cohen

Words, the power of words, is all important.
Words can inspire.
Words can destroy.
There is an insightful Midrash which says, "These are the words." Read *devarim* – words and also *devorim* – wasps.

Words can console us, words can cajole us. Words can tear like wasps at our very flesh.

Be Careful Of Unnecessary Words!

The story is told about the Chofetz Chaim who once visited a generous donor to his Yeshiva. During their conversation the wealthy entrepreneur was busy writing a telegram to a business associate.

After a few minutes of conversation, it seemed that the discussion was leading in the direction such that *Leshon Hara* might ensue. At that point the Chofetz Chaim noticed that the businessman had rewritten the telegram several times, and commented to him about his having written out every word with great care.

The businessman replied that indeed he had taken great care in composing the telegram, since "every unnecessary word here will cost me extra expenses."

The Chofetz Chaim replied: "If only everyone was as careful as this when choosing what to say! Don't they know that every unnecessary word they speak will cost them dearly in the World To Come?"

The midrash says: "Refrain from evil talk and live a life of shalom" *(Derekh Eretz Zuta)*.

Of What Importance Can Mere "Words" Be?

The Rabbis of the Talmud connected the Hebrew for leprosy (*tzaarat*) with the Hebrew words *motzi shem ra* – slanderer, making the assumption that leprosy was a punishment for slander and gossip.

The Talmud has an abundance of advice about care in speech. For example: "Your friend has a friend, and your friend's friend has a friend, so use caution in your speech" (Ketubot 109b).

Rabbi Alexander Zusia Friedman, in his collection of commentaries called *Wellsprings of Torah* brings this comment: One may think: "Of what importance are my words? A word has no substance, neither can it be seen or touched." However, even though words have no substance and are invisible, like the wind they can nevertheless cause entire worlds to crash.

Care With Words, Speech And Prayer

Rabbi Ronald Isaacs, in his book, *Derech Eretz: The Path To An Ethical Life*, reminds us that "The *Amidah* prayer begins and ends with a meditation about words. Its beginning is: "Open my mouth, God, and my lips will speak your praise."

The *Amidah* concludes with the following paragraph: "My God, keep my tongue from evil, my lips from lies. Help me to ignore those who slander me ..."

Rabbi Isaacs reminds us that words are among the most powerful forces in the world. Perhaps we should pay closer attention to the words we pray, especially words in the *Amidah*,

Part Two

Judaism's most central prayer.

Another sage once warned: Be careful what you pray for – your prayers might be answered!

Gossip: Where Do We Start When We Want To Stop?

Like dieting, stopping smoking, and other addictive and unhealthy habits, it is always difficult to start. We can't do it all at once. That never works. That's why most, or all diets fail.

If we want to stop gossiping, and have less to repent for next Yom Kippur in our litany of *Al Chets*, we could not do better than to follow the advice of Joseph Telushkin and Dennis Prager, in their book, *The Nine Questions People Ask About Judaism*.

Their suggested first steps are:
- Eliminate gossip at the Shabbat dinner table. (This holy time should be the first place to avoid speech which is unholy.)
- Avoid spending time with people who are always gossiping.
- Change the topic when others start to gossip.
- Keep private conversations confidential.
- Don't start your gossip diet Monday morning. Start right now!

Judaism Is, Above All, A Love of Language
Rabbi Ismar Schorsch[29]

In a marvelous flourish of Rabbinic fantasy, R. Yosi ben Zimra has God address the tongue directly.

"What else could I have done to rein you in, O tongue of deceit? Though all human limbs are erect, I made you to lie flat. Though all limbs are external and visible, I concealed you inside the body. Moreover, I enclosed you behind two walls, one of bone (the teeth) and one of flesh (the lips)."

In other words, the very anatomy of the organ betrays the

---

29 From The Jewish Theological Seminary website.

Creator's anxiety about its physiology! What motivates this tirade against loose and hurtful language? It is the Rabbinic conviction that the ability to speak makes humankind most God-like.

What was it that God blew into Adam's nostrils at the moment of creation which brought him to life (Genesis 2:7)? For the Hebrew phrase *"le-nefesh hayya* – living being," the oldest Aramaic translation we have, Onkelos suggests "a being that speaks." The added specificity underscores the nature of the endowment. Like God, humankind was to be the only living creature to enjoy the extraordinary power to create through words.

Human speech is a faint echo of the language of God, and to abuse and corrupt it is to assault the essence of our being. It is for this reason that the long and oft-respected public confessional on Yom Kippur, the "*Al Chet,*" devotes at least one quarter of its lists of transgressions to acts of verbal violence.

Judaism is, above all, a love of language, witness the Rabbinic efforts to sanctify it. The way we address each other foreshadows the way we will treat each other. The words of the gifted Russian poet Osip Mandelstam, sent to Siberia by Stalin in the 1930s and murdered by the Nazis in 1941, haunt me: "The word is flesh and bread. It shares the fate of bread and flesh: suffering."

Resist The Temptation
Rabbi Dov Peretz Elkins

A Lesson from Barbara Bush: "I Won't Trash My President"

The other morning while getting dressed I heard Barbara Bush on a morning news show, being interviewed about her new book of memoirs. The interviewer found a passage in the book that Barbara Bush wrote in her diary, which she kept while her husband was President, and which she quotes at length in her book. In that entry she wrote: "I can't imagine that Bill Clinton will ever be President."

Naturally, the interviewer went for the jugular. His question: What was it about Bill Clinton that made you think he could never become President?

Part Two

Barbara, who was much beloved by the American people during her term as First Lady, shot back: "I won't answer that question. George taught me, and I feel the same way: Never trash your President. He's my President, and I won't discuss that any further."

What respect and admiration Barbara Bush must have received from the millions of viewers, people of good will of both parties, who heard her response. She had a chance to spread some juicy gossip, to pounce on this policy or that policy, on this action or that, on some misstep, or fault of character. There were any number of things Barbara could have said, and could have scored points with millions of Republicans, or right-wing conservatives.

But she refused. She wouldn't commit *Leshon Hara*! It's one of the most scurrilous, and yet one of the most easy and popular indoor sports in America today – by the media, by government officials, by politicians, by members of organizations, including Jewish organizations, and including synagogues, people who love to pounce on the president, or the Rabbi. For most people who are human it is easy to cut people up. It gives a temporary charge, like a joint or a needle. But its long-range effects are just as devastating – to ourselves and to others.

Barbara Bush taught us an important lesson. Be strong, and resist the temptation for the momentary high. Consider the long-term effects of the poison that is spread by gossip and carping and unnecessary criticism, and hold your tongue.

Leshon Hara – Negative Speech

Undermining Society
Dr. Stanley Friedland, Psychologist

According to Rabbinic tradition, *tzaraat* (leprosy) in the Torah is caused by slander and gossip. This could not have been a contagious disease; if it were, it would have presented the people of Israel with a serious public health problem.

Many commentators therefore believe that the critically important aspect of leprosy was the isolation of the *metzora* (leper), from the community. The Ramban believed that the leper was separated from society to prevent a repetition of *Leshon Hara,* gossip and slander.

The Maharal of Prague wrote that lepers were isolated because they undermined the peace of society that they had damaged. Other scholars believed that the forced separation from society was an extended "time-out" designed to increase the leper's self-awareness by forcing him or her to think about what he or she had done. The leper's isolation also served to teach members of the community about the power of speech and the dangers of *Leshon Hara.*

Tracking Words Is Harder Than Tracking Money
Anonymous

Hank Eskin is only 34, but like many people his age, he has created an Internet site that is gaining in attention. It's not a money-making project, at least I don't see how, but it is one that is being followed by more and more people who love interacting with the computer screen. His website enables people to track their dollar bills, learning where it continues to go after it leaves their hand. In other words, using the serial numbers printed on all denominations of U.S. money, a person can track their bills as they are reported by other Internet fanatics around the country and even around the world. While the website is very new, it already tracked one bill that was entered six times in and around Kansas and Oklahoma. (USA Today, 8/27/99).

This can be done because the bills carry a serial number, that is one of a kind. Why someone cares where their bills travel, I can't fathom. But I do know that there is something that travels

Part Two

at least as far and passes through as many people as a dollar bill, but cannot be tracked, and certainly not returned and pulled out of circulation. I speak of *Leshon Hara*, gossip, slander, rumors, or as our tradition calls it, evil speech. Once it's out of your mouth and made its way to another's ears, it is gone, never to be retrieved or returned. Oh, you may hear your rumor come back to you from someone else, most likely grown and expanded. But you can't pull it out of circulation. Every time it passed from one person to another it did more damage. And, as the Chofetz Chaim pointed out, it hurt not only the subject of your rumor, but everyone else who heard it. It made them parties to the crime, the crime of destroying another's reputation, and perhaps their livelihood, their family, maybe even their life.

That's why the litany of the *Al Chet* that we recite on Yom Kippur, though it tries to cover every conceivable sin, inevitably are overwhelmed by sins of the tongue. If we commit to changing just this one habit, that of sins of the tongue, Yom Kippur services will have changed our lives tremendously for the better!

Tale Bearing And Evil Gossip
#301 on Maimonides Negative List
Rabbi Jonathan Ginsburg

Leshon Hara is a generic term covering various types of improper speech, including slander and evil gossip. Our tradition actually understands this mitzvah as prohibiting the peddling of gossip even if the report is true. This tradition shows great insight into the destructive power of speech. Here are a few examples from the Torah.

- Joseph is pictured (Gen. 37:2) as having brought an evil report about his brothers to his father. Joseph was punished for his *Leshon Hara*.
- The spies commit *Leshon Hara* against Eretz Yisrael when they return with a report outlining the difficulties in conquering the land (Num. 14:36-37).
- Miriam was troubled by Moses' marriage. Her *Leshon Hara* was punished by an affliction of her skin (Num. 12:1-15).

Leshon Hara is so powerful that, once spoken, it cannot be corrected. This is such a basic concept that we pray for protection against this sin in the meditation at the end of every *Amidah*. Written by Mar ben Rabina and cited in Berakhot 17a, this prayer begins: "My God, keep my tongue from evil, my lips from lies. Help me ignore those who slander me."

According to the Rabbis, *Leshon Hara* kills three: the one who tells it, the one who listens to it, and the one about whom it is told.

When Children Learn To Talk

A Father's Message to His Two-Year-Old Son
Jeff Jacoby, Boston Globe Columnist

It perplexes me that you still aren't talking. But it's not an entirely bad thing. After all, you have never yet told a lie. You have never yet used a bad word. You have never yet uttered an insult or hurt anyone's feelings. You have never yet spread malicious gossip.

Once you start talking, you'll feel the urge almost daily to engage in one or another of these forms of wrongful speech. And – trust me on this, Caleb – it's an urge fiendishly difficult to resist. But resist you must, and part of my job is to help you learn how.

Our tradition places so much emphasis on the importance of avoiding malignant talk. "Who is the man who desires life, and yearns for many days to enjoy prosperity?" asks King David in the 34th Psalm. "Then guard your tongue from evil and your lips from speaking lies."

I know that nothing will influence the words that come out of your mouth more than the words that come out of your parents' mouths. So we are careful about what we say and how we talk in your presence. The Talmud teaches, "What a child says in the street is the words of his father or mother." Eventually you will meet people, maybe even other kids, who resort to crude language or cutting put-downs when they don't get their way. I cannot shield you from such speech forever, but I can try to make sure you never hear it at home.

Part Two

The Twisted Kernel Of Truth
Kirk Douglas, Actor/Author

Some years ago there was a story in the *National Enquirer* about Carol Burnett that depicted her as drunk at a dinner with Henry Kissinger. Carol was incensed. Of course, it wasn't true. She decided to sue. After lengthy and costly legal proceedings, the courts decided that she had been wronged and awarded her damages of $1.6 million. The legal staff of the rag fought and argued, and got it reduced to $200,000 on appeal.

What did Carol win? Her legal fees were over a million dollars. Imagine the time and effort expended. The public rarely sees a retraction. All the public remembers is a story about Carol Burnett being drunk.

Sometimes the stories have a kernel of truth – Carol Burnett did have dinner with Henry Kissinger and wine was served – but the little kernel of truth is twisted and exaggerated into a huge lie.

A Difficult Law To Obey
Kirk Douglas, Actor/Author

While I was studying Torah with Rabbi (David) Aaron, he told me many interesting stories. One that stuck with me was about his ten-year-old daughter. One day she came running home after school.

"Daddy, Daddy, a boy hit me with a spitball in school today."
"He did?"
"Yes, and he hurt me."
"What's the boy's name?"
"I can't tell you," his daughter replied. That would be *Leshon Hara*."

Of course, I had no idea what the child was talking about, until the Rabbi explained it to me.

"Did you ever find out who hit her?" I asked the Rabbi.
He laughed. "No, I never did."
Wow. Can you imagine what would happen in our society if everyone behaved like this little girl? First, people would trust each other, having no basis for suspicion. Second, all gossip would

be out the window. Most newspapers would be very thin. And the tabloids would be out of business. Now *that* would make this a better world.

I must admit it is a difficult law to obey. I myself like a little gossip. Virtue is not photogenic; who wants to read about a nice guy? But there should be some limits, because gossip and rumors spread so quickly, like an epidemic. So much harm is done when millions of people are fed lies, innuendos and half-truths.

One scoop that led to a tragic ending involved the trashing of an American hero, Oliver Sipple, who had saved the life of President Ford. For putting his life on the line and tackling the would-be assassin Sara Jane Moore, Oliver Sipple asked just one thing of the press: Please grant me my privacy. By the time the media was through digging up all the dirt on him, that he was gay, his family had disowned him, his mother was dead, and finally Sipple himself committed suicide.

The stuff the media reported about Sipple may have been true, but so what? He was dead.

Rabbi (Joseph) Telushkin has proposed a Speak No Evil Day and even got a bill introduced in the U.S. Senate, but as of this writing the measure is stalled, probably because all election rhetoric would have to be suspended for that amount of time. And aren't politicians always running for office? Is there a time that would be safe for them?

Words Are More Like An Arrow Than A Sword
Rabbi Donald B. Rossoff[30]

Rabbi Joseph Telushkin, in his wonderful book *Words that Hurt, Words that Heal,* makes the point that unless you or a close one have been the victim of some terrible physical violence or catastrophic illness, chances are the worst and most lasting pains you have suffered in life have come from words used cruelly – from ego-destroying criticism, excessive anger, sarcasm, public and private humiliation, hurtful nicknames, betrayal of secrets, rumors

---

30   Rabbi Donald B. Rossoff has been a congregational Rabbi for 39 years and is completing a Masters degree in marriage and family therapy.

Part Two

and malicious gossip.

Do you remember Oliver Sipple? Mr. Sipple was that ex-Marine who saved President Ford's life from a would-be assassin in San Francisco and became a national hero. Reporters badgered him about details of his life, but he asked them not to get into that. Well, inquiring minds wanted to know, and so the *L.A. Times* reported that Sippel was involved in many gay rights organizations, which was why, in 1975, he asked that his personal life be kept personal. His family back in Detroit cut him off. He was not allowed at his mother's funeral. He began to drink, became withdrawn, and was found dead in his apartment a few years later. "If I had to do it over again," said the *L.A. Times* reporter, "I would not have broken the story."

Words are more like an arrow than a sword. A sword, when it leaves the sheath, can be put back in the sheath. An arrow, once it leaves the bow, cannot be called back.

Words Are Holy
Rabbi Sidney Greenberg

The confessional on Yom Kippur lists forty-four sins for which we ask to be forgiven. Of these, no fewer than ten are sins of speech.

The terrible thing about the malicious word is that it is so irretrievable. An old Jewish story tells of a woman who came to her Rabbi on a wintry day with a terrible sense of guilt. She had spread a very unkind story about another woman in the town, and had just learned that the story had no basis in fact whatsoever. What should she do?

The Rabbi told her that she would have to do two things. First, she would have to take the feathers from one of her pillows and place one feather on the doorstep of each of the houses in the little town. After she completed this task she should return and the Rabbi said he would give her a second task.

The woman left and returned the following day. "What shall I do now?" she asked.

"Now," said the Rabbi, "go gather up all the feathers from each of the houses where you put them."

"But Rabbi," protested the woman, "that is impossible. The wind has already scattered them far and wide."

"Indeed, it has," said the Rabbi. "To gather up those feathers is as impossible as to take back the harsh words you spoke. You would do well to remember that before you speak in the future."

The tongue is in a very wet place and it is so easy for it to slip. And how often do we inflict with our tongue the kind of blows which burn deeper and hurt so much longer than any physical blows we can inflict.

Dr. Paul Tournier, the Swiss psychiatrist, tells of a woman he treated. She was experiencing a distressing sense of unworthiness and emptiness in her life. After a period of counseling the patient recalled a telling incident from her childhood. She had been in another room and overheard her mother say to her father about her: "We could have done without that one." That careless remark had twisted a life out of shape.

Many of us who wouldn't dream of lifting a hand against another human being, think nothing of inflicting damaging blows with our tongues. When we were kids there was a popular ditty which we used to defend ourselves against verbal onslaughts: "Sticks and stones will break my bones, but names will never harm me."

We don't believe that anymore. Nor do we believe one of the cynical slogans of our time: "words are cheap."

A bride and groom under the canopy, betting their lives on each other and summing up this fateful decision in a few words, do not believe that words are cheap.

A young man being interviewed by a prospective employer for a position for which he has prepared himself over long, hard years, does not believe that words are cheap.

A lawyer pleading desperately for the life of his client does not believe that words are cheap.

Children gathered around the bedside of a dying father, who is leaving his last verbal legacy, do not believe that words are cheap.

At such moments surely words become freighted with an urgency and a decisiveness which leave their permanent imprint upon human lives. At such critical junctures we accept the judgment of our tradition that "Life and death are in the power of the tongue."

But Judaism goes beyond these spectacular and dramatic moments. It tells us that at all times, in every circumstance, words

Part Two

are holy. For it is in this God-given power to speak, to utter syllables and to frame them into intelligible means of communication with other people that we have one of the truly distinguishing human traits which separates us from the beasts.

In medieval Jewish philosophy, man is called *medaber,* "the one who speaks," for it is this faculty which differentiates us from the rest of the animal kingdom as well as from the world of nature.

What care should, therefore, be exercised in our manner of using words! Who does not know their fateful power.

Three times a day, at the end of each *Amidah,* we pray: "O God, keep my tongue from evil and my lips from speaking deceit." A mensch constantly guards the tongue and the lips because words are holy.

The Terrible Gossiper

Do you know the story about the four ministers who came back to school for a class reunion? They were sitting around reminiscing, and one of them said: "You I can tell. I have a terrible temptation to steal. When the collection plate goes around, if no one is looking, I reach in and I take some of the money for myself."

The second minister said: "You I can tell. I have a terrible temptation for women. And sometimes, in the middle of the service, when I look out, if I see an especially beautiful woman, I have lascivious thoughts."

The third minister said: "You I can tell. I have a terrible temptation for strong drink. And sometimes, when no one is looking, I take the wine from the communion cup, and drink it myself."

And then the three of them turned to the fourth classmate and they said: "And you?"

The fourth minister answered: I'm a terrible gossiper, and I can't wait for this meeting to be over."

Death and Life are in the "Hand" of the Tongue
Rabbi Prof. David Golinkin[31]

A professor at the Jewish Theological Seminary once came home after officiating at a synagogue during the High Holy Days and said to his teacher, Rabbi Simon Greenberg (z"l): "Professor Greenberg, I simply can't take the *Al Chet* anymore! Forty four sins repeated nine times – it's just too much!"

And Prof. Greenberg replied: "Of course it is! I haven't said them all for years."

The professor was taken aback. Could it be that his teacher, who was such a genuinely pious person, had not recited the *Al Chet* in years?

"What do you mean?" he asked.

"It's very simple," said Prof. Greenberg. "Each time I choose one of the sins on the list, one that applies to me. I think about its implications and meditate on how and why I committed it – and by the time I am finished thinking about that one sin, the rest of the people have finished the whole list."[32]

This is very good advice. Jewish law requires us to confess our sins at every service on Yom Kippur,[33] but we are not required to say the exact list of *Al Chet*, which has grown steadily longer throughout the centuries.[34] Therefore, as a way of preparing for Yom Kippur this year, I would like to zero in on two of the *Al Chet* phrases connected to speech. Indeed, ten of the 44 phrases, almost one quarter, refer to sins committed through speech. Among other things we say:

- *For the sin we have committed before You by the utterance of our lips.*
- *And for the sin we have committed before You in the speech of our mouths.*
- *For the sin we have committed before You by impure lips.*
- *And for the sin we have committed before You by the*

---

31 David Golinkin, *Insight Israel: The View from Schechter*, second series, The Schechter Institute of Jewish Studies, Jerusalem, 2006, pp. 28-37.

32 Rabbi Jack Riemer, *The World of the High Holy Days*, Miami, 1991, p. 301.

33 Yoma 87b.

34 See the Rema to Orah Hayyim 607:2.

Part Two

foolishness of our mouths.
- *For the sin we have committed before You by slander.*
- *And for the sin we have committed before You by tale bearing and gossip.*

Gossip and Slander

The first four verses are a general confession of our mouth's ability to sin, but the last two verses refer to two specific commandments mentioned numerous times in the Bible and Talmud and codified by Maimonides. They are called *Leshon Hara*, which means slander, and *rechilut* or *rechilus*, which means tale bearing or gossip.

The basic prohibition against *rechilut* or gossip is already found in the Torah: "Do not go about as a talebearer among your countrymen ... I am the Lord."[35]

What exactly is a *rachil*, a talebearer? Rashi explains[36] that it comes form the word *rochel* or peddler: just as a peddler peddles merchandise from one house to another, so a talebearer or gossip carries overheard information from one person to another. [37]

Many centuries later, the book of Proverbs[38] condemned another kind of sin committed by the mouth: "He who spreads slander is a fool."

In Rabbinic literature, slander is called *Leshon Hara*, which literally means "the evil tongue." The Rambam defines *Leshon Hara* as a person who says bad things about his fellow man even if he is telling the truth.[39]

The Rabbis of the Talmud and Midrash ranked *Leshon Hara* among the worst types of sin. They said: "Slander is worse than the three cardinal sins of murder, forbidden sexual relationships and idol worship."[40]

"Whoever tells *Leshon Hara*, God says of him: 'He and I cannot

---

35 Leviticus 19:16.
36 Ibid.
37 Cf. Yerushalmi Peah 1:1 and Rambam, Hilkhot Deot 7:2.
38 Proverbs 10:18.
39 Hilkhot Deot 7:2.
40 Tanhuma Metzora, par. 4 = Midrash Tehillim 52, ed. Buber, p. 283 = Arakhin 15b.

Leshon Hara – Negative Speech

inhabit the same world'."[41]

"Whoever slanders deserves to be stoned."[42]

"Because there are slanderers in this world, I have removed My presence from among you."[43]

"Whoever slanders has no place in the world to come."[44]

Furthermore, the Rabbis emphasized the fact that a number of prominent Biblical figures were severely punished for the sin of *Leshon Hara*: Ten of the twelve spies sent by Moses to spy out the land of Israel slandered *Eretz Yisrael*. As a result, they were punished by death.[45]

Miriam, the sister of Moses, uttered *Leshon Hara* against Moses because of his Ethiopian wife. As a result, God punished Miriam with leprosy.[46]

As you may know, Moses himself was not allowed to enter the "promised land" because when God told him to bring forth water from the rock by speaking to it, he struck the rock instead.[47] However, according to Rabbi Simone, he was not punished for striking the rock, but rather because he called the Jewish people "*hamorim* – rebels." In other words, Moshe was severely punished for speaking *Leshon Hara* against the Jewish people.[48]

Lastly, one sage did not allow his colleague to slander a certain Jewish community – even though his remarks were probably true. In Talmudic times, Caeserea was known as a city of assimilated, Greek-speaking Jews. As a matter of fact, the Jews there were so assimilated, that they used to recite the *Shema* in Greek, because they did not know Hebrew![49]

The midrash relates that Rabbi Abbahu and Resh Lakish were entering the city of Caeserea. Said Rabbi Abbahu to Resh Lakish: "Are we allowed to enter a city of cursing and blasphemy?"

Resh Lakish dismounted from his donkey, gathered some sand, and stuffed it into Rabbi Abbahu's mouth.

41 Arakhin 15b.
42 Ibid.
43 Devarim Rabbah 5:14, ed. Mirkin, pp. 106-107.
44 Pirkei Derabi Eliezer 53, fol. 127a.
45 Numbers 14 and Arakhin 15a.
46 Numbers 12.
47 Numbers 20.
48 Shir Hashirim Rabbah to 1:6, ed. Vilna 9a.
49 Yerushalmi Sotah Chap. 7, fol. 21b.

Part Two

Rabbi Abbahu exclaimed: "Hey, what are you doing?"

Resh Lakish replied: "God is not pleased with one who utters slander against the Jewish people!"[50]

Thus far we have seen that *rechilut* or gossip and *Leshon Hara* or slander are forbidden by Jewish law. We have also seen that these sins were the subject of Rabbinic hyperbole, and that even Biblical figures were roundly criticized by our Sages for the sin of *Leshon Hara*.

Words Can Kill

But why? What's so terrible about a little gossip or *rechilut*? What's wrong with some harmless slander or *Leshon Hara*? After all, doesn't the children's ditty say: "Sticks and stones will break my bones but words will never harm me"? Children may believe that ditty, but adults know better. Not only can words harm, they can kill! This is even evident from the idioms for slander in various languages. In English it's called "character assassination." In Biblical Aramaic it's called "*akhalu kartzeihon di*",[51] which literally means "they ate the flesh of...". And the medieval Hebrew poet Moshe Ibn Ezra wrote: "a talebearer is like a cannibal."[52]

The deadly power of our tongues is emphasized in a famous verse from Proverbs (18:21): "*Mavet v'hayyim beyad Leshon* – Death and life are in the *hand* of the tongue", upon which the Talmud[53] comments: "Does the tongue have a *hand*? This comes to teach us that just as the hand can kill, so can the tongue kill."

Another Rabbinic dictum takes this analogy with murder one step further: "A person who slanders, kills three - the teller, the listener, and the victim."[54] The Sages derived this from the story of Doeg the Edomite who told King Saul that Ahimelekh the Priest helped David. This *Leshon Hara* led to the death of Doeg the teller, King Saul the listener, and Ahimelekh the Priest whom Doeg had slandered. However, this teaching need not be taken so literally. Even when they do not kill, *Leshon Hara* and *rechilut* destroy the

50   Shir Hashirim Rabbah to 1:6, fol. 9b.
51   Daniel 3:8, 6:25.
52   Shirat Yisrael, ed. Halper, 1924, p. 40.
53   Arakhin 15b.
54   Midrash Tehillim 52, ed. Buber, p. 284 and ibid. 120, p. 504 and parallels.

character of the teller, the listener, and the victim. The devastating power of our tongues is illustrated by two stories from our own day:

Dr. Paul Tournier, the Swiss Psychiatrist, tells of a woman he treated. She was experiencing a distressing sense of unworthiness and emptiness in her life. After a period of counseling, the patient recalled a telling incident from her childhood. She had been in another room and overheard her mother say to her father about her: "We could have done without *that* one!" That one bit of *Leshon Hara* had twisted her entire life out of shape.[55]

The second story is well known to all of us. In 1995, right-wing demonstrators in Israel began to call Prime Minister Yitzhak Rabin z"l a *boged*/traitor and a *rodef*/pursuer on a regular basis. Rabin himself dismissed this kind of talk as nonsense. Yet, there is no question that these "mere words" – *boged* and *rodef* – influenced Yigal Amir and contributed to the assassination of Prime Minister Rabin.

Slander is Irretrievable

In addition to its destructive power, there is another reason why Jewish tradition is so opposed to *Leshon Hara* – slander cannot be retrieved. Once uttered, it has a life of its own. It spreads like wildfire in every direction and cannot be controlled. This point is emphasized in a very powerful *midrash* on two verses from Psalms (120:3-4). The verses read: "What can you profit, what can you gain O deceitful tongue? A warrior's sharp arrows...". The *midrash* comments:

"The tongue is compared to an arrow. Why? Because if a person draws a sword to kill his fellow man, the intended victim can beg mercy and the attacker can change his mind and return the sword to its sheath. But an arrow, once it has been shot and begun its journey, even if the shooter wants to stop it, he cannot."[56]

Our tongues are like arrows – once we have shot off our mouths in slander and gossip, our words proceed to destroy the victim's character and there is nothing we can do to stop them. Or, as another *midrash* on those same verses states: "So it is with

---

55 Rabbi Sidney Greenberg, Lessons for Living, Bridgeport, Conn., 1985, p. 93.

56 Midrash Tehillim 120, ed. Buber, p. 503.

slander; it is uttered in Rome and kills in Syria."[57]

The irretrievable nature of *Leshon Hara* is clearly illustrated in the following story:

A woman came to her Rabbi on a wintry day with a terrible sense of guilt. She had spread a very unkind story about another woman in town, and had just learned that the story had no basis whatsoever in fact. What should she do?

The Rabbi told her that she would have to do two things. First, she would have to take the feathers from one of her pillows and place one feather on the doorstep of each of the houses in the little town. After she completed this task, she should return and the Rabbi would give her a second task. The woman left and returned the following day. "What shall I do now?" she asked. "Now," said the Rabbi, "go gather up all the feathers from each of the houses where you put them."

"But Rabbi," protested the woman, "that is impossible. The wind has already scattered them far and wide." "Indeed, it has," said the Rabbi. "To gather up those feathers is as impossible as to take back the harsh words you spoke. You would do well to remember that before you speak in the future.[58]

Some Other Pernicious Effects

Slander and gossip have a number of other pernicious effects. Frequently, they destroy lifelong friendships. As the medieval proverb states: "If you believe all the gossip around you, you will be left without one good friend."[59]

In addition, even when you scoff at *Leshon Hara* and dismiss it as sour grapes, it still leaves a residue. This is brought home by an Aramaic proverb found in the *midrash*: "If slander does not wholly penetrate the listener's heart, at least it fills half of it."[60] Thus, even when not taken seriously, slander has a pernicious effect on the listener.

Furthermore, slander and gossip frequently backfire; the perpetrator becomes the victim. This phenomenon is described

---

57 Bereishit Rabbah 98:23, p. 1269.
58 Rabbi Sidney Greenberg, Lessons for Living, pp. 92-93.
59 Reuven Alkalay, Words of the Wise, no. 1811; Israel Davidson, Otzar Hameshalim V'hapitgamim, no. 369.
60 Bereishit Rabbah 56:4, p. 599.

in an oft-quoted medieval Hebrew proverb. One version says: "Whoever speaks against other people, other people will speak against him." Another version says: "He who slanders others for things they have not done, will be slandered in turn for things he has done."[61]

Lastly, *Leshon Hara* ultimately serves no purpose. The slanderer has harmed his victim but gained nothing in return. That is why the Talmud compares a slanderer to a poisonous snake – it kills others with its bite but derives no benefit from that act.[62]

How can we eliminate gossip and slander?

We have seen that *rechilut* and *Leshon Hara*, gossip and slander, kill the teller, the listener, and the victim. They are irretrievable and unstoppable. They destroy friendships, they frequently backfire, and ultimately they are pointless. Clearly, then, the family, the Jewish community, and society as a whole will benefit, if we make a concerted effort to eliminate *rechilut* and *Leshon Hara* from our lives. But how do we do so? Isn't that a pretty tall order? Yes it is, but the solution is really quite simple: we must stop *Leshon Hara* at both ends of the line – the telling end and the listening end.

The need to stop telling *Leshon Hara* can be neatly summed up in a proverb attributed to Rabbi Yisrael Salanter, the famous nineteenth-century moralist. He said: "Jews must be as careful about what comes out of their mouths as about the food that goes into their mouths."

The other method, however, is not so obvious: The other way to stop gossip and slander is to refuse to listen to it. We all have a natural tendency to gravitate toward gossip and slander. This tendency is expressed in the quip attributed to Alice Roosevelt Longworth: "If you haven't got anything good to say about anyone, come and sit by me." It is also evident in Norman Rockwell's painting "The Gossips", first published in 1948. In it, a tidbit of gossip is transmitted from mouth to mouth by fourteen people. If any of those people had just said "no", the gossip would have been stopped dead in its tracks. But, in each case, listening to the gossip

---

61 Israel Davidson, Otzar Hameshalim Vehapitgamim, no. 1402.
62 Arakhin 15b.

Part Two

led to that person *telling* the gossip to someone else.[63]

That is why the Talmud says: "If a person hears something unseemly, he should put his fingers in his ears!"[64] In the fourteenth century, Eliezer ben Shmuel Halevi of Mainz admonished his children in a similar fashion: "Do not stand next to slanderers, because if not for the receivers and believers of *Leshon Hara*, people would not tell *Leshon Hara*."

We shall conclude with three classic pleas for controlling our tongues: [65]

1. The first is found in Psalm 34:13-14 and is recited every Shabbat and holiday morning in the Psalms of Praise:
Who is the man who desires life,
who desires years of good fortune?
Guard your tongue from evil,
and your lips from deceitful speech.

2. The second passage is a story found in *Leviticus Rabbah*,[66] which is based on the verse just quoted:

A story is told of a peddler who was making the rounds of all the towns near Tzippori and announcing: "Who wants to purchase the elixir of life? – Let him come and take!" He entered the town of Akhbera and approached the house of Rabbi Yannai who was sitting and studying in his dining room. Rabbi Yannai heard the peddler announce: "Who wants to purchase the elixir of life?" He looked out at him and said: "Come up here and sell it to me." The peddler retorted: "Not to you nor to anyone like you." Rabbi Yannai persisted and the peddler went up to him and took out the Book of Psalms and showed him the verse, 34:13: "Who is the man who desires life" and the verse which follows "Guard your tongue from evil."

---

63 Christopher Finch, Norman Rockwell's America, New York, 1975, figure 19.
64 Ketubot 5a-b.
65 Israel Abrahams, Hebrew Ethical Wills, Philadelphia, 1926, p. 215.
66 16:2, pp. 349-351.

3. The last passage is found in the Talmud (Berakhot 17a) and is recited after the *Amidah* three times a day, all year long:

O Lord,
*Guard my tongue from evil
and my lips from speaking guile.*

This, then, is our challenge in the year ahead: to avoid spreading gossip and to refuse to listen to *rechilut*; to stop slandering our fellow man and to close our ears to *Leshon Hara*. If we do so, we will have happier families, a more peaceful Jewish community, and a healthier society.

Bibliography
I) Primary Sources
1) Bialik and Rawnitzki, eds., *Sefer Ha'aggadah*, Tel Aviv, 1947 and reprints, pp. 543-546 (also available in English)
2) Israel Al-Nakawa, *Menorat Hamaor*, ed. Enelow, Vol. 4, New York, 1932, Chapter 18, pp. 337-370
3) Yehudah Moriel, *B'derekh Tovim*, Jerusalem, 1985, Chapter 6, pp. 102-115
4) Rabbi Moshe ben Maimon, *Mishneh Torah, Sefer Mada, Hilkhot Deot*, Chapter 7 (also available in English)

II) Secondary Sources
1) *Encyclopaedia Judaica*, s.v. Leshon ha-ra and s.v. slander
2) Greenberg, Rabbi Sidney, *Lessons for Living*, Bridgeport, Connecticut, 1985, pp. 92-94
3) Hakohen, Rabbi Yisrael Meir, *Sefer Hafetz Hayyim*, Vilna, 1873 and reprints
4) Idem, *Sefer Shemirat HaLeshon*, Vilna, 1879 and reprints
5) Hurwitz, Simon, *The Responsa of Solomon Luria*, New York, 1938, pp. 95-99
6) Pliskin, Zelig, *Guard your Tongue: A Practical Guide to the Laws of Loshon Hara based on the Chofetz Chayim*, New York, 1975
7) Potok, Rabbi Chaim, *The Ethics of Language*, LTF, New York, 1966, 17 pp.
8) Telushkin, Rabbi Joseph, *Words That Hurt, Words That Heal: How to Choose Words Wisely and Well*, New York, 1996
9) www.WordsCanHeal.org/articles/InsightSeptember2003

Part Two

Positive Word Power
Rabbi Zelig Pliskin

What kind of a human you will be depends largely on how you utilize the greatest gifts the Creator gave you: Your ability to think and speak.

Every time you speak to another person you have a choice to make: What should I say to this person right now and how should I say it? A wise and kind choice of words will elevate you and enable the person you are speaking with to feel good in the present and will help build his self-image.

It is a great misuse of this awesome gift to cause other people pain with your words. The Talmud states that it is a worse crime to cause pain with words than to cheat another person financially. Why? Money can be returned. Words, once said, can never be taken back. The harm and damage of insults and putdowns can last for a lifetime.

When you insult someone and cause distress with your words, you are striking against the dignity of the other person. The highest level of kindness is to build someone's self-image. For the same reason, the worst crime is to rob someone of self-esteem and lower their self-image.

Most people aren't totally aware of the great harm they cause when they make destructive and demoralizing statements and when they hurt others with offensive and disrespectful speech. It's so easy to make counterproductive comments and ask non-constructive questions. There are many forms of subtle negative statements.

Very few people are truly mean and sadistic. But everyone gets frustrated, even angry at times. These feelings are the breeding ground of comments that hurt and inflict pain.

Ask any counselor or therapist and you will hear of the great damage caused to children who were insulted by their parents and teachers, siblings and peers, friends and neighbors. The unseen scars of hurtful words cause pain and anguish over and over again.

Ask any marriage counselor and you will hear of the mutual damage and pain caused to husbands and wives by the painful statements that were said out of frustration and anger. Even the nicest people speak in ways they shouldn't when they are in a bad mood.

Leshon Hara – Negative Speech

What is the solution to this problem of epidemic proportions? We must all gain a greater awareness of what we are actually saying. Fortunately there is a new tool on the market that will give us the awareness we all desperately need.

The Chofetz Chaim Heritage Foundation has recently produced an amazing book, *Positive Word Power* (Artscroll). It is a very practical and fascinating guide to the Torah's wisdom on human interaction arranged for daily study.

If you speak to others, you need to read this tremendous book. One reading of the book will already give you a deeper and heightened awareness of the power of your words. You build a better world with the words you speak when you speak wisely and kindly. You destroy lives when you do the opposite.

Everyone who reads this book will recall times when others caused them pain with what they said. Hopefully this will serve as a motivator to be more careful from now on with what we say.

Every parent and teacher needs to read this. And so does every husband and wife. And so does every brother and sister. And so does every neighbor and classmate. And so does anyone who buys or sells. And so does anyone who asks questions to another person or needs to answer the questions of anyone else. To put it concisely: If you speak to others, you need to read this tremendous book. Everyone you speak to will be glad you did.

Our emotional states have a tremendous impact on what we say and how we say it. After reading this book, I gained greater awareness that:

- When we are hungry and tired, we need to be especially careful with how we speak.
- When we feel frustrated in an interaction with someone, we must be careful to avoid sarcastic remarks.
- When we are angry at someone and feel like letting him know how we feel, we need to master the self-control necessary to speak in a way that will express our true concerns without belittling or shaming the other person.
- When we are involved in an argument with someone, we need to remember to remain calm and centered and to continuously speak in ways that are an expression of mutual respect.
- The most important (and hardest!) point to keep in mind is: "Think before you speak!"

Part Two

The Leprosy Of Irresponsible Speech
Rabbi Bradley Artson

Learning to control our speech will enable us to transform the world into a community that respects the shared humanity of all people.

In the Torah, we learn a great deal about the ritual function of the *Kohanim* (priests) in helping people cope with infectious illness. Particularly the illness of *tzaraat* (leprosy), becomes the focus of sustained attention, presumably because it was quite common in the ancient Near East.

Basing themselves on a story found in the Book of Numbers, the Rabbis of the Midrash viewed leprosy as an external sign of an internal decay. Illness became a symbol for corruption, immorality and callousness.

The link between illness and a lack of ethics arises from the story of Miriam's criticism of Moses' wife for being a Cushite. Clearly, Miriam uses her sister-in-law's ethnicity as a pretext for attacking her brother. Whereas Jewish tradition goes so far in rejecting racism that the Rabbis of the Midrash and Talmud justify Moses' selection of an African woman as his wife, Miriam is unable to restrain her harmful comments and her corrosive bigotry.

In a condemnation that neatly parallels Miriam's criticism that Moses' wife is too black, Miriam is stricken with an illness that leaves her skin a flaky white. Since her *tzaraat* resulted from her critical words, the Rabbis naturally associated the two.

Thus, the Biblical laws on infectious disease became an extended metaphor for self-centeredness, critical or slanderous speech, and hateful deeds.

Things God Hates

Midrash Vayikra understands the law of leprosy as an allusion to seven traits the Lord hates:
- haughty eyes
- a lying tongue
- hands that shed innocent blood
- a heart that devises wicked thoughts
- feet that run eagerly toward evil

- a false witness
- one who sows discord among people

How many of these violations pertain to an irresponsible use of language!

Speaking and thinking ill of another person, construing their actions in the worst possible way, gossiping and spreading rumors which harm the reputation of another person – these activities are so widespread among our contemporaries that they no longer attract our notice at all. Yet they strike at the core of the kind of world Judaism is trying to establish. Those practices provoke a cynical disregard of human decency; they cultivate our suspicion of each other and our assumption that others are speaking ill of us behind our backs just as we are of them.

In Hebrew, such speech is called *Leshon Hara* (literally, "an evil tongue"). *Leshon Hara* is the practice of speaking about other people, rather than speaking to them. It involves transforming a living, complex human being into a caricature – an object of evil, or sloth, or competition. In speaking ill of others, we participate in their dehumanization, initiating a process whose end is uncontainable.

Sensitivity To Speech
Rabbi Jordan D. Cohen

Rabbinic interpreters regarded leprosy as punishment for the sin of careless speech.

Overview

The Torah portions of *Tazria* and *Metzora* are perhaps, for many, the two most uncomfortable portions of the Torah, dealing with all kinds of issues related to ritual purity and impurity.

Ritual impurity, or *tumah*, has nothing to do with hygiene. Instead, *tumah* is a spiritual state that prevents a person from participating in the worship life of the community. One becomes impure through a variety of means, all of which are perfectly natural, such as illness, childbirth, physical discharges and contact with a corpse.

Part Two

Purity and impurity are not related to good or evil. However, impurity is considered to be a spiritual disability. For example, *tzaraat*, the skin affliction that is discussed at length in this part of the Torah, is not the biological disease leprosy (as it has historically been translated – it is probably something more like psoriasis or impetigo, which are common in the desert) but rather a state that the Torah understands as the physical manifestation of a spiritual or ritual problem.

This is not a medical treatise, nor are the Kohanim (priests) serving as paramedics. Rather, *tumah* is a purely ritual concern, and as the ritual leaders of the community, it falls upon the priesthood to facilitate purification for those who find themselves in a state of impurity.

In Focus

And God spoke to Moses, saying, "This shall be the law of the *metzora* (one afflicted with *tzaraat*) on the day of his purification; he shall be brought to the Kohen (priest)" (Leviticus 14:1).

Pshat

In *Parshat Metzora*, the Torah discusses the process of purification the *metzora* must undergo in order to become ritually pure again.

Drash

The late Rabbi Pinchas Peli (z"l) relates the following tale: In the town of Sepphoris, the voice of a street peddler was heard, crying out, "Who wishes to buy the elixir of life?" The great Rabbi Yannai was sitting in his academy studying when he heard the peddler's voice. He went out on his balcony to see what it was the man was selling, but he could see nothing. And so he sent one of his students to bring the peddler to his study.

As the peddler entered, Yannai said, "Come here, show me what it is that you have to sell."

The peddler replied, "What I have to sell is not required by you, nor by people like you."

But the Rabbi pressed him, and finally the peddler approached him and drew a Book of Psalms out of his satchel. He opened the

Leshon Hara – Negative Speech

book and showed the Rabbi the passage that states, "Who is the man who desires life?" (Psalm 34:13), and then the passage that follows immediately thereafter: "Keep your tongue from evil; depart from evil and do good."

Rabbi Yannai then said, "All my life I have been reading this passage, but did not know how to explain it until this peddler came and made it clear to me. Now I see that the same idea is also expressed by King Solomon, who proclaimed in a proverb, 'He who guards his mouth and his tongue guards his soul from trouble' " (Proverbs 21:33).

Who are they who desire life? They who keep their tongues from evil. The one who guards his mouth and his tongue guards his soul from trouble.

When we look at the historical setting of this story, in Palestine in the early third century, we can see that this story is not just a simple little moral tale. The Land of Israel at this time was in turmoil. There were revolts and insurrections against the Roman conquerors. Roman spies and informers were everywhere, constantly on the watch for clues of rebellion.

The peddler, in his surreptitious manner, was passing the word that everyone should be wary of what they say. In a good Jewish manner he was passing the word: "loose lips sink ships." Rabbi Yannai, by responding with his own remarks, indicated his support for this clandestine effort. He reiterated the message: those who desire life, those who want to survive these oppressive times, should watch their words.

It is interesting though to see the context in which this midrashic story is presented (Vayikra Rabba 16). It is presented in a commentary on the laws of *tzaraat*, which are presented in our Torah reading this week. The laws of the *metzora* have long been the basis for numerous Rabbinic homilies against the spread of *Leshon Hara* – literally "evil speech" or gossip. *Metzora*, the Rabbis conjectured, sounded just like *motzi shem ra* – the bringing forth of evil with the mouth. Cause and effect: if one is guilty of *Leshon Hara*, one will be afflicted by *tzaraat* and thus becomes a *metzora*.

But the Torah tells us that *tzaraat* is not a permanent condition. One can become healthy again. Neither the condition, nor the sin that precipitated it, is hopeless. There is always the possibility of *teshuva* – expiation for one's misdeed – and a process by which the unclean *metzora* could again become pure and rejoin the community. This process always exists for us, no matter what our sin.

Also implicit in this verse is the thought that the *metzora*, even while he is still outside the camp, should be impelled by his own free will to repent and come to the priest in order to be cleansed. It is only in response to his personal resolve to become pure that he should be taken to the priest and thus brought closer to the state of purity.

Only after the *metzora* has decided to take positive action leading to repentance and purity, shall "the priest go forth out of the camp" to cleanse him. People must rise to actions themselves before they can expect action from above. (*Shem MiShmuel*)

The Drive-By Sin
Rabbi David Wolpe

We are deluged by rumor, gossip, tall tales masquerading as truth. Good names are sullied and reputations ruined at the careless push of the "Send" button. In an age of loose talk, Jewish teachings on improper speech have never been more important.

Life and death, Proverbs proclaims, are in the power of the tongue. The ancient Aramaic translation of the Torah refers to human beings as "the speaking animal."

In Genesis, God creates the world through words. Words not only create a world, but they can destroy it too – sabotaging relationships, betraying friendships, hurting others both close and faraway.

All the usual excuses – "That's just what I heard"; "I didn't mean it unkindly"; "But it's true!" – are clumsy dodges by which we allow ourselves the fleeting pleasure of being "in the know" while doing lasting harm. Gossip is the drive-by sin; once the damage is done, we are already gone.

Rabbi Joseph Telushkin reminds us of three questions we should ask before passing on tales: Is it true? Is it fair? Is it necessary? If not, then don't repeat it. God credits us for what we say and also for what we resist saying.

Smooth and Deceptive Language
Maimonides

You are forbidden to accustom yourself to use smooth and deceptive language. Do not say one thing when you mean another, but let your inner thoughts be in accord with the impression you give; say what you really think. Even one word of smooth talk or misrepresentation is forbidden; you should, rather, have truth on your lips, a sincere spirit, and a heart free of trickery and deceit.

Rumors: Is It Appropriate to Pass One On?
Rabbi Joseph Telushkin[67]

The Jewish tradition sets a very high bar for considering a rumor worthy of being transmitted.

While all moral people would agree that spreading a malicious and untrue story about another person is vile, almost everyone of us, including me, has done so – most, many times. When? When we routinely pass on rumors.

Most rumors are not positive and complimentary. ("Hey, did you hear that so-and-so is really a wonderful person?"). Rather, many, if not most rumors are negative and often untrue as well. If you pass on a rumor that turns out to be both ("I heard that Michael was fired from his last job because he was caught embezzling"), you have helped cause serious damage to another person's reputation, and inflicted possibly irrevocable damage. Jewish law categorizes such behavior as *motzi shem ra* (giving another (literally "spreading") a bad name), and regards it as a particularly vicious offense.

People who transmit reputation-destroying rumors often defend themselves by claiming, "But I didn't do it on purpose. When I spread the rumor, I thought it was true." Such a defense is analogous to a drunk driver who has caused a fatal accident saying, "But I didn't intend to kill anyone." Of course he or she didn't, but so what? That a person was killed because of negligence, and not on purpose, is scant consolation to the victim's family. Similarly,

---

67   Reprinted from *The Book of Jewish Values*, published by Bell Tower.

the fact that the person who passes on an ugly rumor thinks that because it is true in no way minimizes the harm inflicted on the rumor's object.

Therefore, how careful should we be to verify a rumor's truthfulness before we transmit it as fact? The Talmud[68] suggests the following guideline: "If the information is as clear to you as the fact that your sister is forbidden to you as a sexual mate, (only) then say it."

How hard is it to comply with such a standard? Very; the one consolation is that offered by the sage Ben Sira: "Have you heard something? Let it die with you. Be strong; it will not burst you."[69]

But is such a standard too restrictive? For example, what if a friend tells you that he is going to invest money with someone whom you have *heard* has a poor track record as a financial manager? Or if you have *heard* that your friend's job is at risk? Or if you learn that an acquaintance is consulting a physician whom you have *heard* is incompetent?

Some might argue that since you do not know for a fact that the negative details you have heard are true, you should say nothing. Others, myself included, feel that saying nothing does not seem morally right. After all, does your lack of definitive knowledge require you to stand by and wait for your friend to lose money, or to become a victim of malpractice?

There is an intermediate moral position, one that neither permits the random spreading of rumors nor categorically forbids passing on rumors you don't definitively know to be true: to warn your friend of what you have heard, but not claim that what you are telling him or her is established fact. For example, in the case of the money manager, say to your friend something like this: "Before you invest money with so-and-so, make sure that you check with several others who've invested with him. I've heard his track record is spotty. I don't know this for a fact, but it would be naive to dismiss out of hand what one has heard people say."

By emphasizing that what you have heard is hearsay, and that your friend should first investigate the matter, you protect the potential investor while avoiding, to the extent possible, damaging the reputation of the person being discussed.

---

68   Babylonian Talmud, Shabbat 145b.
69   Apocrypha, Ben Sira 19:10.

Professor Michael Berger, who is also an ordained Rabbi, is not fully comfortable with the solution I've proposed: "In my view, making the sort of comment you suggest is appropriate only if the other person will do due diligence and check out the person. But if your friend's reaction to your 'warning' is 'I don't need this headache,' and just dumps the person, then, if you have heard these rumors from a possible slanderer, (to choose one example) you become complicit in ruining the financial manager's livelihood. It seems to me that the right thing to do is to insist that your friend check the person out because it's the *prudent* thing to do – and not because of something you have heard."

What Jewish tradition teaches us is that even when it comes to passing on a rumor, there is an ethical – and an unethical – way to act.

Our Weapons Of War
Rabbi Ya'aqob Menashe

There is a parable of a king who had many servants. Among them was a group who were strong and courageous and would make powerful warriors. The others were much weaker and would not be fit for such an undertaking. The king separated these two groups and gave the powerful ones bows and arrows and other weapons of war and taught them the skills of how to succeed in battle.

What did the servants do? They took their weapons and roamed the city streets and markets, marauding, injuring and killing innocent people who had the misfortune of being at the receiving end of their weapons. When the king heard of this, he brought them all to judgment. He said to them, "Before I separated you from the others, you were equal in all respects. The only advantage that you had was that I gave you weapons and taught you the art of war. By doing this damage you have made yourselves inferior to the others."

We should learn from this that God separated man from the animals. He gave us a tongue that can shoot arrows, which are the study of the Torah and our prayers which serve as weapons against our enemies. If, however, a person uses his God-given gift, which is

Part Two

his tongue, for inappropriate speech, such as *Leshon Hara*, he is effectively shooting arrows in the King's city, against those whom He loves and against all that is holy.

God's purpose in separating us from the animals was so that we would raise ourselves to a much higher level, but not to become inferior to them. It behooves us to remember this at all times, and use our speech for holy and appropriate purposes.

The Local Gossip Queen
Anonymous

Betty, the local gossip queen, and self-appointed monitor of the neighborhood's morals, kept sticking her nose into other people's business.

Several neighbors did not approve of her extracurricular activities, but feared her enough to maintain their silence.

She made a mistake, however, when she accused George, a new neighbor, of being an alcoholic after she saw his old pickup truck parked in front of the town's only bar one afternoon. She emphatically told George (and several others) that everyone seeing it there would know what he was doing.

George, a man of few words, stared at her for a moment and just turned and walked away. He didn't explain, defend, or deny. He said nothing.

Later that evening, George quietly parked his pickup in front of Betty's house ... walked home ... and left it there all night.

You gotta love George.

Uncontrolled Appetites
Rabbi Michael Gold

"The Lord spoke to Moses saying, This shall be the ritual of the leper at the time that he is purified, when it has been reported to the priest."[70]

---

70   Leviticus 14:1-2.

Leshon Hara – Negative Speech

I heard a troubling report on National Public Radio (NPR). The segment spoke of a non-profit organization that ran a small gift shop to raise funds. The gift shop was manned by volunteers. The head of the organization discovered that the gift shop was earning far less than expected. Both gift items and cash were disappearing. The organization thought there was a thief involved. But when they put some controls on the cash and merchandise, they discovered that many of the volunteers were helping themselves to items. A gift here, a little bus fare there – people justified it because they believed they were volunteering. With accounting controls, the stealing stopped.

The NPR report went on to say that people, given the opportunity, often cannot resist the temptation to take something that does not belong to them. We all have an appetite to take things. Security cameras and laws prevent us from following our appetites. Without such deterrents, many of us follow our appetites. In Jewish tradition, we have a name for our appetites out of control. We call it the *Yetzer Hara*, usually translated the "evil inclination." We all have such an inclination.

Last week when I was in Las Vegas, I realized why it is called "sin city" and why it is so popular. The whole city is built around people losing control of their appetites. The Rabbis at the convention could not walk to their daily prayer services and Torah study sessions without passing through the casinos. Why not put a little into the slot machines before putting on a tallit? The casinos are one of the last indoor places in the United States where smoking is not only permitted, but is the norm. We all know about the free drinks offered to big spenders. Then there are the all-you-can-eat buffets of food and the sexy shows. Vegas is the perfect place to let your appetites take control.

Do not misunderstand me. I enjoyed my stay there. It is a fun city. But it is vital that anyone who goes there has a strong sense of self-control and knows his or her limitations. We call that the *Yetzer Hatov* or "good inclination." But as anyone who has ever struggled with addictions can testify, self-control is a hard virtue to develop. Temptation may be prevalent in Vegas, but it exists everywhere.

There is one area of life where virtually everybody loses control of their appetite every day. We all love to gossip. That is

Part Two

the reason why gossip magazines and television shows have such a huge following. That is the reason why so many young people get caught up speaking ill about fellow students. And that is the reason why Facebook and other social networking sites often become places of bullying and nasty talk about one's "friends."

This week's Torah portion once again speaks about a skin disease called *tzaraat*, usually mistranslated "leprosy." We do not know exactly what the disease is. But the Rabbis noted the similarity between the name of this disease and the phrase *motzi shem ra*, "speaking evil about others." They claim that this disease is a punishment for evil gossip. They brought proof from the Biblical story of Miriam, who spoke evil about her brother Moses' wife and broke out with this disease. According to the Rabbis, what starts out on our tongue eventually breaks out on our skin.

Rabbi Joseph Telushkin, a well-known author and lecturer, tried to get Congress to pass a resolution calling for one gossip-free day a year. I doubt many of us, whether in Congress or not, could live up to that ideal. I often ask the teens in my synagogue, "Could you make it through a whole day without speaking evil about anybody?"

Most admit, "Only if I spent the whole day in bed by myself."

We all have appetites. One of our most powerful is the appetite to gossip. Perhaps the solution is, whenever we hear something negative about someone else, say something positive. In a small way, this would make the world a better place.

Metzora: Slander and its Comeuppance
Moshe Sokolow

Tzaraat, the subject of this week's portion (and, in part, of last week's as well), has traditionally been translated as leprosy, a word seemingly derived from the Greek *lepra* (scales). Contemporary translators, reluctant to use the word, either substitute a euphemism like "skin blanch" (Robert Alter) or retain the Hebrew term (Everett Fox). In a parallel context, the World Health Organization has replaced "leprosy" with "Hansen's disease."

What lies behind this reticence? Biblical *tzaraat* simply doesn't meet the specifications of leprosy, defined by the National Institutes of Health as "an infectious disease characterized by disfiguring skin sores, nerve damage, and progressive debilitation." Not only, as Robert Alter notes, do the symptoms not correspond, but "there is scant evidence that leprosy was present in the Near East before the Hellenistic period."

Besides, if *tzaraat* were infectious, treatment would call for isolating the sufferer the instant he presented the first signs or symptoms. Yet the procedure delineated by the Torah allows for a postponement of the "diagnosis" for a week or even two, and the Talmud notes that prospective sufferers were not even examined during the major festivals when, arguably, the population density of Jerusalem – and the risk of contamination – was at its highest. Finally, whereas Hansen's disease is diagnosed by a dermatologist and treated with antibiotics, *tzaraat* was diagnosed by a priest and was not so much treated as "purified" by means of a ritual.

So if *tzaraat* was not leprosy, what was it? Aryeh Kaplan, a distinguished American Orthodox Rabbi and scholar, defined it as "a physical symptom of a spiritual defect." What kind of defect was it; why was *tzaraat* an appropriately punitive sign of its presence; and how did the prescribed ritual ameliorate the condition?

One way to determine the etiology of the disease is by reference to individuals in the Bible who were afflicted by it. Among well-known personages, the first was none other than Moses, whose hand briefly turned "*tzaraat* as snow" at the Burning Bush.[71] Another was Moses' sister, Miriam, who was similarly stricken "*tzaraat* as snow"[72] and spent a week in isolation. What did the

---

71 Exodus 4:7.
72 Numbers 12:10.

Part Two

two have in common?

It was not so much what they had as what they did: namely, according to Talmudic tradition, engage in slander (*Leshon Hara*). Moses maligned the Israelites by suggesting they were likely to disavow his Divine mission; Miriam impugned Moses' prophetic standing. Indeed, the Talmud not only views *tzaraat* as punishment for slander; it views it as retributive justice. As slander is the moral equivalent of murder, *tzaraat* is a figurative death penalty. A Talmudic idiom designates slander as "blanching another's face in public" – an appropriate verbal metaphor for the physical appearance of *tzaraat*: as pale and as snow-white as death.

Similarly, just as slander offends the social order, *tzaraat* entails enforced social ostracism, enfeebling the offender while he contemplates his error. This, the commentators point out, is manifest in the ritual prescribed in the Torah for purifying *tzaraat*: "They shall take for the one being purified ... a piece of cedar wood, a scarlet thread, and a clump of grass."[73] Rashi (1040-1105) explains: "*Cedar wood*: Because afflictions are caused by arrogance (the cedar being known for its loftiness). *Scarlet thread and grass*: What is the antidote? He must humble himself like a thread and a clump of grass."

Jewish practice no longer marks out *tzaraat* as a disease – and no longer imposes isolation on slanderers. But the need is at least as great now as it was back then to take social responsibilities seriously and view interpersonal relations as, figuratively, a matter of life and death.

Rabbi Abraham Isaac Kook is reported to have said that if the destruction of the Second Temple was due to gratuitous enmity and jealousy, the way to redemption lay through gratuitous friendship and affection – a timely thought for the approaching Jewish festival of freedom and redemption.

---

73 Leviticus 14:4.

Leshon Hara – Negative Speech

Guard That Which Comes Out Of Your Mouth[74]

The Holy Jew of Peshischa instructed his student Rabbi Simhah Bunim to take a trip, but did not explain the purpose. Rabbi Bunim took with him several Hasidim and began the journey. They came to a certain village, and wanted to eat with one of the residents of the village. The resident informed them that he did not have any dairy products in the house, but had only meat. The Hasidim began to investigate the level of kashrut, such as who was the *shohet* (ritual slaughterer), whether the animal had been a kosher one, and whether the salting procedures had been carried out properly.

While they were questioning the resident in these matters they heard a beggar call out to them, "Hasidim, Hasidim! What you place *in* your mouth you inquire about – whether it has been *kashered*, and how it has been *kashered*. But what comes *out* of your mouth – the words you utter – about them you ask no questions, and do no intensive inquiry."

When Rabbi Simhah Bunim heard the words of the guest, he understood why the Holy Jew had sent him: in order to learn this important lesson from the passing stranger. He then returned home immediately.

The Power Of Words
Letitia Elizabeth Landon, a 19th century British poet

'Tis a strange mystery, the power of words!

Life is in them, and death. A word can send
The crimson colour hurrying to the cheek.

Hurrying with many meanings; or can turn
The current cold and deadly to the heart.

Anger and fear are in them; grief and joy
Are on their sound; yet slight, impalpable –
A word is but a breath of passing air.

---

74 Tales of the Righteous, ed. Simcha Raz, trans. Dov Peretz Elkins.

Part Two

The Greatest Sin – Sinning Against One's People

Rabbi Yitzhak Elhanan Spector of Kovno taught: See how great is the sin that one commits against one's people!

From the Torah we learn that the Blessed Holy One forgave the generation of the wilderness for many great sins that they committed against Him.

They sinned with the golden calf. They were forgiven.

They sinned in lusting to eat meat. They were forgiven.

They sinned again in the quarrel of Korah. Again they were forgiven.

Only for the sin of the spies – when they brought a bad report on the Land of Israel, and asked to return the people to Egypt – God did not forgive the Israelite people. God decreed regarding those who left Egypt: "In this very wilderness will your carcasses fall."[75]

From this we learn that of all the sins in the world – both sins between humans and God and sins between humans and their neighbors – repentance will remove the sin.

Only for the sin that one sins against one's people, there is never atonement. Even if one should have complete and total regret and does total repentance – there is no atonement for such a grievous sin!

Feathers in the Wind
Rabbi Yechiel Eckstein

When anyone has a swelling or a rash or a shiny spot on their skin that may be a defiling skin disease, they must be brought to Aaron the priest or to one of his sons who is a priest.

Leviticus 13:2

The Torah portion for this week is a double reading, *Tazria-Metzora*, from Leviticus 12:1-15:33 and the Haftorah from 2 Kings 7:3-20.

Anyone who has ever spent time at the school or neighborhood

---

75 Bamidbar 14:29.

playground has undoubtedly heard this retort before: "Sticks and stones may break my bones, but names will never hurt me." However, anyone who has been verbally abused can tell you, it's simply untrue. While kids can learn to recover from such verbal assaults, the fact still remains: *words can hurt.*

Most of this week's Torah reading centers around a spiritual malady that presents itself as a physical disease. It is a disease that can affect a person's possessions, home, and eventually, body. The person who is afflicted with such a disease is called a *metzora* in Hebrew. The term is a contraction of three other Hebrew words: *motzi shem ra*, which means "spoke badly about another person." This reveals the crime of the afflicted – one who uses words to harm another person.

While we know words can be hurtful, is the offense really that bad? After all, words are just words. Sure, they may sting for a moment, but then they are gone with the wind. Aren't they?

A story is told about a man who went around slandering the Rabbi of his town. After some time, the man regretted his actions and asked the Rabbi for forgiveness, saying he would do anything to make amends. The Rabbi told him to take a pillow and open it up in order to let the feathers scatter in the wind. The man did as was told and then returned to the Rabbi. The Rabbi said, "Now go and collect all of the feathers." The man replied, "But that's not possible!" Then the Rabbi made his point: "And so it is with words. Once they leave your mouth, it is impossible to retract them and who knows how far they will spread."

This is why the Bible views the sin of speaking badly about others as such a serious offense, even equating it to a disease. Words are compared to arrows; once shot, their direction is no longer in our control, and their effect can be deadly. The tongue is so powerful a weapon that God created two gates to contain it – one is our teeth, the other our lips. We need to carefully consider our words and think before we open our mouths to speak. After all, broken bones can heal, but hurtful words go on forever.

Part Two

Listening and Filtering
Dr. Erica Brown

The call of the Jewish people and our central tenant of faith demands that we listen: "Hear, O Israel, the Lord Our God, the Lord is One." Pay attention. Attune your ear. Hear and be responsive. At the same time, we have to be conscious of what we should *not* be listening to, what we must close our ears from hearing.

In Deuteronomy, we learn that when cleaning up after ourselves in the wilderness, we are obligated to use a shovel. A playful Talmudic reading of this verse reads that our fingers should serve as shovels or stoppers in our ears when we hear gossip or slander.

"Bar Kapara said: What does it mean 'You shall have a '*yated*' (shovel or peg) in addition to '*ozenecha*' (your tools)? Don't read the word, '*ozenecha*' but rather '*aznecha*' (your ear). If a person hears something improper being discussed, he should place his fingers in his ears."

God conveniently gave us fingers that could serve as the right size stoppers against malicious talk. We have to use them.

Every day, our ears take in so much information. We use them to hear words of praise and study, instruction and advice, information and judgment. We all make selective decisions about what we hear and how we listen. The ears are a precious filter. In this season of personal growth, we might consider a new "ear workout" – to strengthen both this listening and filtering muscle.

Guard Your Tongue
Rabbi Yechiel Eckstein

"They make their tongues as sharp as a serpent's; the poison of vipers is on their lips."

Psalm 140:3

Winston Churchill's composure, especially in the face of opposition, was legendary. A story is told about him that occurred during his last year in office. Churchill took his seat at an official government ceremony when he overheard two men sitting several

Leshon Hara – Negative Speech

rows behind him whispering: "That's Winston Churchill. They say he is getting senile. They say he should step aside and leave the running of the nation to more dynamic and capable men."

When the ceremony ended, Churchill turned around to the men and said, "Gentleman, they also say he is deaf!"

In his witty way, Churchill was teaching the men that not everything they hear is true. However, this story also demonstrates that most people do believe everything they hear, whether it is true or not.

Speaking slander, *Leshon Hara* in Hebrew, is taken very seriously in the Bible. The Sages teach that when people gossip, they violate no less than 31 Biblical commandments. The most classic commandment against slandering can be found in Leviticus 19:16: *"Do not go about spreading slander among your people."* In Biblical times the offense of slander was considered so great it was met with the harsh punishment typically meted out for leprosy, and included a week of isolation.

Why is slander dealt with so harshly?

The answer can be found in Psalm 140, which is entirely about being a victim of slander. In it, the psalmist prays for Divine protection from evildoers who *"make their tongues as sharp as a serpent's; the poison of vipers is on their lips"* (v. 3). The psalmist calls slanderers "violent" and "wicked." He describes their evil words as a trap set to ensnare him.

Unlike the childhood rhyme, "Sticks and stones may break my bones, but names will never hurt me," the psalmist does not see these hurtful words as harmless. As any victim of slander or bullying can attest, words can be as harmful as a trap, and as deadly as venom. This is why we are to avoid them at all costs. Just as we must be vigilant with a loaded gun, we must guard our lips and mouths, which are just as powerful.

The good news is that the Sages also teach that one who holds back from speaking words of gossip or slander earns a spiritual reward beyond comprehension. God gave us two gates – our teeth and our lips – to help us guard our tongues and use them properly. Recently I came across this helpful tip: **THINK** before you speak: Ask, is it **T**rue? Is it **H**elpful? Is it **I**nspiring? Is it **N**ecessary? Is it **K**ind? If the answer is no to any of the above, close the gates and lock them.

Part Two

Guard That Which Enters And Leaves Your Mouth
Rabbi Yisroel Jungreis

Leshon Hara is the equivalent of all three cardinal sins – a concept which might be difficult for us to absorb. In the 21st century, gossip has become a profession. Newspapers employ gossip columnists. Gossip columnists have social cachet and are very much sought after by hostesses and the media, and some of the biggest bestsellers are based on gossip.

Our Torah laws are like a beacon of light that illuminates our path and reminds us of our higher calling. Speech is a Divine gift, given only to man. To abuse that gift is to betray that trust.

To what extent we must go to avoid *Leshon Hara* can be learned from Miriam, the prophetess, who in good faith criticized her younger brother Moses, and for those seemingly innocent words, was afflicted with *tzaraas*. The Torah commands us to *remember* what happened to Miriam and be cautious with our words even when we believe that we are speaking for the benefit of another.

Meet the Evil Inclination
Rabbi Eli Scheller [76]

When you will go out to war against your enemies...
Deut. 21:10

This week's Torah portion begins with various laws concerning warfare. Our sages tell us that the opening verse is hinting at going out to war against our most fearsome enemy – the evil inclination.

As the Chovos Halevavos writes:

Your greatest enemy in the world is your evil inclination. He gives you (bad) advice every step of the way. While you sleep he is awake, plotting against you. He appears to you as a friend, and he becomes one of your most trusted advisors... His greatest weapons against you are confusion and false arguments, which make you forget your true interests and doubt your confirmed goals and beliefs... (Shaar Yichud Hamaaseh).

---

76   www.aish.com

Leshon Hara – Negative Speech

The evil inclination always has something up his sleeve and never gives up. The Rebbe from Peshische said that a person should imagine the evil inclination as one who is standing over his head with an axe, waiting for the perfect moment to chop off his head.

Rabban Gamliel was once traveling in a boat when he saw that another boat was sinking. He noticed that Rabbi Akiva was one of the passengers on board. Mourning over the great loss, he got to shore and walked into a nearby shul. He was shocked to see that the one giving the lecture was none other than Rabbi Akiva! Astonished, he cried out, "Akiva, how did you get here? I saw you drowning!" Rabbi Akiva replied, "As I was drowning a wooden plank from the boat was floating right by me. I quickly stuck out my hand and grabbed on to it. It kept me above water. As each wave came, I put my head under the water until it passed, and then I kept on going." [77]

The Maharal explains that the waves were an allusion to the evil inclination. Rabban Gamliel saw that Rabbi Akiva was getting swept away by the evil inclination and was drowning in the sea of life. Rabbi Akiva replied that he grabbed on to the wooden plank – he grabbed on to the Torah which is referred to as the tree of life, and that saved him from drowning!

The only sure way to beat the evil inclination is by studying Torah. As the Talmud states: God created the evil inclination and created the Torah as its antidote.[78]

Rumor Has It
Dr. Erica Brown

Local gossip lasts for a day and a half.
BT Moed Katan 18b

First things first. How's your 30-day Elul challenge going? Let's put another challenge out there: 30 days gossip-free.

The English singer Adele has a great song called "Rumor Has

---
77 Yevamos 121a.
78 Kedushin 30b.

Part Two

It." It's an expression we recognize that takes out the human element. We're not spreading rumors. Rumors do their own work, as Adele's lyrics suggest:

All of these words whispered in my ear,
Tell a story that I cannot bear to hear,
Just 'cause I said it, don't mean that I meant it,
Just 'cause you heard it.

Words whispered in her ear remind me of one of my oft-quoted saying from Proverbs 18:8. It captures the danger of rumors best: "Words of gossip are like delicious morsels; they go down to the inmost parts."

Gossip is delicious but a moment on the lips is forever on the hips in a different way. That piece of malicious or maligning information goes "down to the inmost parts." We cannot erase what we know. We will think of that gossip virtually every time we look at or encounter a person when we know his or her secret failing or weakness.

Another problem with gossip is that the person spreading the rumor does not take accountability for it; he or she may just be passing it along. What's the harm in that? Just because someone said it or you heard it, does not give the statement authenticity. Then what does a rumor accomplish if it may not be true?

A rumor is like a dab of glue that joins people together in secret knowledge that bestows false power over its "victims." Rumors travel quickly and spread so far that they may become impossible to stop or contain. Thus are we warned in Leviticus about not being a talebearer, which literally in the Hebrew is rendered as someone who travels with gossip.

Some people love to be in the know; it's a form of control. They love passing on news about people. "Did you hear...?" They don't want to know that you already heard. They want to be the one to tell you. In Jewish law, gossip does not need to be false to be gossip. It can be true and still be mean-spirited and thoughtless.

The Talmud considers what stops rumors and what spreads rumors and concludes that rumors stop if they are disproven. They gain fuel if no one puts an end to them. When I came across the Talmudic statement above – "Local gossip lasts for a day and a half" – I laughed out loud. The sages actually thought about how long rumors circulate. They concluded that a day and a half is "referring to a rumor that stopped." In their observation of group dynamics, some kind of community self-monitoring takes place that quells a rumor and kills it.

How seriously should you take a rumor, therefore? "A rumor that does not stop must be taken seriously only if a person has no enemies. But if he has enemies, then it was the enemies who disseminated the rumor." In other words, the Talmudic conclusion is that we do pay attention to rumors that do not stop because at heart we assume that good and honest people who live in community with each other will behave with decency and stop unwarranted gossip. If it persists, we need to investigate the truth of the matter. But if the person who is the subject of the rumor has enemies, we dismiss the rumor altogether. Why be part of someone else's negative agenda?

While it would be wonderful to believe that we are high-minded enough to focus on ideas and not on people, we know the powerful draw of rumors, the delicious morsel that is fed into our ears and goes down to our inmost parts and lodges there. That morsel can quickly turn into indigestion. To avoid what we'll call "irritable scowl syndrome" – a general bad feeling about humanity that lives in the gut – we need to make sure that we don't take joy in passing on rumors and certainly think twice before spreading them without investigating their accuracy, as the Bible reminds us: "Do what is just and right."

Shmirat Halashon – Avoiding Gossip
Rabbi Joshua Hammerman

Judaism believes that words have great power. After all, the world was created through words. Language is a gift that should be used wisely. Gossip is dangerous and takes many forms, including malicious slander, unintentional slips of the tongue and even swearing (both in terms of cursing and in taking false oaths). Long before the invention of email, the Rabbis believed that a gossiper in Babylonia could kill someone in Rome.

Cursing:
What does it mean to curse God's name? If, as we read in

Part Two

Genesis, every human being is created in God's image, that Divine part of us is the essence of our humanity. To insult God is to debase our own innate godliness, our human capacity for goodness and kindness. Sometimes curses can be a creative way of dealing with powerlessness. We see that in the colorful Yiddish curses that have sprung up. And Jews have had good reason to shake their fist at the heavens. When Job's wife implores, "Curse God and die," Job has every reason to do just that – but he refuses to, recognizing that God's blessings and curses are intertwined. In fact, the very word translated as "curse" in Job 2:9 is "*barekh*", which also means to bless. Job refuses to render God one-dimensional, the source only of evil and not of life's blessings too. That's what cursing does. It turns God into a stereotype. Once "bleeping" becomes your only way of expression, you are unable to communicate creatively, to probe the complexity of deeper feelings.

Gossip:

Once on the High Holidays, I challenged the congregation to go from Rosh Hashanah to Yom Kippur without gossiping. No one could do it. It's impossible. But everyone became much more aware of what they were saying, which is really the goal of the laws of gossip.

It is our good fortune that the greatest champion of sacred speech that the Jewish world has ever known lived only a century ago. Rabbi Israel Meir Kagan was also known as the Chofetz Chaim, the Seeker of Life, after a book he wrote with that title. Kagan was the first to systematize the laws of gossip for a popular audience. He died in 1933, which is just about when everything began to go awry for the civilized world. Now, as distilled by the Chofetz Chaim, here is how Jewish law instructs us to clean up our use of language:

- It is considered *Leshon Hara*, evil speech, to convey a derogatory image of someone even if that image is true and deserved. A statement that is not actually derogatory but can ultimately cause someone physical, financial or emotional harm is also *Leshon Hara*.
- It is *Leshon Hara* to recount an incident that contains embarrassing damaging information about a person, even if

- there is not the slightest intent that s/he should ever suffer harm or humiliation.
- *Leshon Hara* is forbidden by Jewish law even if you incriminate yourself as well.
- *Leshon Hara* cannot be communicated in any way shape or form, for instance through writing, verbal hints, even raised eyebrows. When that person you can't stand turns away and you roll your eyes in disgust to a third party, that is a form of slander known as *"Avak Leshon Hara,"* the residue of evil speech.
- To speak against a community is a particularly severe offense.
- *Leshon Hara* cannot be related even to close relatives, even to your spouse. The columnist Dennis Prager argues that this goes too far, saying, "If you never speak about other people with your partner, you're probably not very intimate with each other." Telushkin suggests that if we are going to gossip we should develop a way of talking about others that is as kindly and fair as we would want others to be when talking about us.
- Even something that is already well known should not be repeated. Even the latest lurid Washington scuttlebut or Hollywood scandal. We still can't talk about it unless that information has a direct bearing on the well-being of the person we're talking to.
- Tattling is a no no. This is called *Rechilut* in Hebrew. The crux is this: if you know that a person has spoken badly about your friend, you don't go to your friend and tell him, because all it does is cause him pain and provoke animosity between the friend and that other person. Well, you ask, shouldn't we have a right to hear what's being said about us? In practice, however, the one small piece of gossip transmitted often provides a totally false impression. Who here has never said a negative thing about the person you love the most? How devastating it would be for a so-called friend to tell our loved one about it. Mark Twain said, "It takes your enemy and your friend, working together, to hurt you to the heart; the one to slander you and the other to get the news to you."

Part Two

- And finally, not only does Judaism prohibit the spreading of *Leshon Hara*, we can't listen to it either. And when we can't help but hear it, we are instructed not to believe it. Imagine how different our lives would be if everybody gave the victim of gossip the benefit of the doubt.

The Tongue As Sword
Dr. Erica Brown

Reckless words pierce like a sword, but the tongue of the wise brings healing.

Proverbs 12:18

This week, the United States Supreme Court heard arguments in a case about the use of threatening language. The case revolves around Anthony Elonis, who is estranged from his wife and posted threats on his Facebook page using the form of rap lyrics after she left him and took their two children. He said he would kill her, shoot up a school and slit the throat of an FBI agent. One Biblical verse kept coming to mind for me as I learned more about the case: "Reckless words pierce like a sword, but the tongue of the wise brings healing."

The language Elonis used was graphic and violent: "There's one way to love ya, but a thousand ways to kill ya..." and then the language gets more painful until Elonis concludes that "Revenge is a dish that is best served cold with a delicious side dish of psychological torture." His estranged wife received a restraining order but this did not stop him. A week later, he posted this message, among others: "Fold up your protective order and put it in your pocket. Is it thick enough to stop a bullet?"

Lawyers defending Elonis say that he was merely venting his hurt and frustration over the split up and had no intent to act on any of these threats. The language he used is not different from the lyrics of many rap singers today and the language content of many violent video-games, raising a question with huge implications. What constitutes free speech and what constitutes an illegal threat in the age of Cyberspace? The government is arguing that it does not matter what Elonis intended if his language would feel threatening to a "reasonable" person, the way the federal court generally determines if a verbal threat is violent. What's under question is what constitutes a standard because free speech is a First Amendment right. You may not like what someone says, but it does not mean that he or she is not free to say it in this country.

This argument gets to the heart of language itself. Justice Ruth Bader Ginsburg asked the momentous question of the bench: "How does one prove what's in somebody else's mind?" You can only really judge people by what they say. Yet in an age where we exaggerate and use expressions of violence in non-violent ways all of the time, it is increasingly difficult to determine the veracity of language: "I could kill for that hamburger right now." "Slay me." "If I say that again, shoot me."

It will be fascinating to see how the court rules this summer on this case.[79] In the meantime, the case should make us all a little more sensitive to language and its intentions. Words can heal. They can also pierce like a sword. Even when the sword is removed, the scar remains. I find at moments like this, a tour of some other verses in Proverbs provides solace:

"A soft answer turns away anger, but a harsh word stirs up wrath"

Proverbs 15:1

"The tongue of the wise speaks knowledge, but the mouth of fools pour out folly"

Proverbs 15:2

"Whoever keeps his mouth shut and his tongue silent keeps himself out of trouble"

Proverbs 21:23

"Whoever guards his mouth preserves life; one who one who opens his lips wide comes to ruin"

Proverbs 13:3

"Do you see a man who is hasty with his words? There is more hope for a fool than for him"

Proverbs 29:20

---

79   Summer 2015; comment on the court's decision, which will be before High Holidays 2015, D.P.E.

Part Two

If you could carry around one of these verses in your wallet to remind you of the responsibilities and perils that come with language, which would it be? Perhaps it would be this verse from Psalms 19:14, the one that is uttered before we begin the Amida, "Let the words of my mouth and the meditation of my heart be acceptable in Your sight, O Lord, my Rock and Redeemer." The mouth represents speech. The heart represents intention. When words and intention are well-aligned in goodness, the words that come out of us bring more healing and beauty to the world. We shouldn't be satisfied with anything less.

When Words Don't Amount To Anything
Thomas Edison

One day I overheard the teacher tell the inspector that I was "addled" and it would not be worthwhile keeping me in school any longer. I was so hurt by this last straw that I burst out crying and went home. I told my mother what these two people were saying about me.

It was then I found out what a good thing a good mother is. My mother came out as my strong defender.

Mother love was aroused, mother pride wounded to the quick. She brought me back to the school and angrily told the teacher that he didn't know what he was talking about, that I had more brains than he himself, and a lot more talk like that. In fact, she was the most enthusiastic champion a boy ever had, and I determined right then that I would be worthy of her and show her that her confidence was not misplaced.

Leshon Hara – Negative Speech

Gossip And Talking About Others
Rabbi Joseph Telushkin[80]

Jewish law goes well beyond secular law in this arena, and forbids the telling of a negative statement about another person, even if it is true.

While libel and slander, which involve the transmission of untrue statements, are universally regarded as immoral and generally illegal, most people regard a negative but true statement made about another as morally permissible. Jewish law opposes this view.

The fact that something is true doesn't mean it is anybody else's business. The Hebrew term for forbidden speech about others, *Leshon Hara* (literally, "bad tongue"), refers to any statement that is true but that lowers the status of the person about whom it is said. Thus, sharing with your friends the news that so-and-so eats like a pig, is sexually promiscuous, or is regarded by her co-workers as lazy, is forbidden, even if true.

Admittedly, this standard is sometimes difficult to observe: The Talmud itself concedes that virtually everyone will violate the laws of ethical speech at least once a day.[81] Nonetheless, those who make an effort to practice these regulations will find that they soon start speaking about others in a far fairer manner.

When it comes to gossip, most of us routinely violate the Golden Rule, "Do unto others as you would have others do unto you." For example, if you were about to enter a room and heard the people inside talking about you, what you probably would least like to hear them talking about are your character flaws or the intimate details of your social life. Yet, when we speak of others, these are the things we generally find most interesting to discuss.

There are times when it is permitted to relate detrimental information about another, but they are relatively rare. While the fact that something negative is true might serve as a defense against a chance of libel or slander in a court of law, it is an invalid defense against the charge that you have violated an important Jewish ethical law.

---

80 Reprinted from *The Book of Jewish Values*, published by Bell Tower.
81 Babylonian Talmud, Bava Batra 64b-65a.

Part Two

Why Refraining from Leshon Hara is an Important Challenge

I know a woman who loved shrimp. When she married a religiously observant Jew, she gave up eating this Biblically forbidden shellfish, and became an observant Jew. Several years later she commented to her husband that she felt irreligious because she still craved shrimp. "On the contrary," he told her, "the fact that you want to eat shrimp, but refrain from doing do because it's prohibited, is proof of your religiosity. The Rabbis teach that one should not say, 'I loathe eating pig,' but rather 'I do desire it, yet what can I do, since my Father in heaven has forbidden it?'"[82]

Rabbi Abraham Twerski, a psychiatrist, wisely observes that this Rabbinic dictum no longer applies to Jews who were raised in ritually observant households. For example, the woman's husband never expressed a desire to eat shrimp. Had he done so, he would probably have become nauseous. The prohibition against eating forbidden foods has become so internalized among observant Jews that refraining from such foods no longer requires any self-sacrifice.

But there is one commandment that almost all observant– and non-observant–Jews are tempted to violate: the ban against speaking *Leshon Hara*. Many otherwise observant Jews frequently violate this Biblical prohibition. They would do well to update the Rabbinic quote to read, "One should not say, 'I do not like to gossip,' but rather, 'I really enjoy talking about and listening to the intimate details of other people's lives, and discussing other people's character flaws, but what can I do, since my Heavenly Father has forbidden it?'"

Adopting this attitude will not only lead to a diminution in gossiping, it will also, as Twerski argues, offer a powerful lesson of true religiosity to one's children. He advocates cutting short a discussion at the dinner table because it is becoming gossipy, and explaining to your children that you are tempted to continue the discussion, but that such conversations are forbidden by God. By doing that, you can demonstrate to your children "by living example the negation of (your) will to that of a higher Authority. It may well be one of the few lessons they'll never forget."

---

82 Sifre Bemidbar, 20:26.

Leshon Hara – Negative Speech

Speech – Use It, Don't Abuse It
Rabbi Eli Scheller [83]

If a tzaraas affliction will be in a person...

Lev. 13:9 [84]

Leshon Hara is a very serious sin and results in the transgressor being afflicted with *tzaraas*, a leprosy-like illness. Why is the sin of *Leshon Hara* so severe that it must be punished with *tzaraas*?

The Torah states, "And (God) blew into his nostrils the soul of life; and man became a living being" (Bereishis 2:7). Onkelos translates "a living being" as a "speaking spirit." Accordingly, it is the soul that gives a person the power to speak. Because the soul and the ability to speak are directly connected, great damage is done to the soul when someone sins through speech. *Leshon Hara* is therefore punished severely and instantaneously.

Rabban Shimon ben Gamliel once sent his servant, Tavi, to buy "good food." Tavi, who was famous for his wisdom, brought back a tongue. Thereupon, Rav Shimon sent him to buy some "bad food." Again he returned with a tongue. Rav Shimon asked him to explain how the same food could be both good and bad.

Tavi answered, "From a tongue can come good and bad. When a tongue speaks good, by complimenting or praising another, there is nothing better. But when a tongue speaks evil, when it tells *Leshon Hara* or makes fun of people, there is nothing worse. It can break up families and kill.

The verse states, "Death and life are in the hands of the tongue" (Mishlei 18:21). The tongue is mightier than the sword. A sword can only kill someone nearby, whereas words spoken on one continent can "hit the heart" of someone on another continent. The tongue, of all the limbs and organs, moves with the least difficulty and most speed. Consequently, *Leshon Hara* is one of the sins committed most frequently. It is for this reason that the mouth is guarded with two gates: the teeth and the lips. A person has to think twice before he says something once. A bird that escapes may be caught again, but a word that escapes will never return!

---

83 www.aish.com
84 Vayikrah Rabbah 33:1.

Part Two

The Power of Thought and Speech [85]

God instructed Moses to tell the Jewish people, "You must not go around as a gossip-monger."

Leviticus 19:16

According to the Talmud, gossip "kills" three people: the speaker, the listener, and the object of the gossip. That the speaker and listener deserve to be punished is understandable, but why should the person about whom they are gossiping suffer?

The answer is that speaking about another person's shortcomings does more than just belittle him. Words have the power to bring latent energy into actuality. When we speak about a person's negative traits, it activates them and reinforces them. As a result, his behavior takes a turn for the worse and he thus incurs punishment.

Conversely, when we speak about the good traits of another person, we reveal and reinforce those traits. We can thus be a positive or negative influence on people; the choice is ours.

It is not only prohibited to speak derogatorily about someone, it is also prohibited to think about them derogatorily. In some ways, thinking negatively about someone is more serious than speaking negatively about them.

Soft Words
Dr. Erica Brown

"Rabbi Joshua ben Levi said, 'A person should never utter an ugly word.'"

BT Pesakhim 3a

As the presidential elections advance, the use of harsh and hostile language has intensified to an unbearable pitch, leading one viewer to tell a candidate that she would not allow her nine-year

---

85 Excerpted from *Daily Wisdom: Inspiring insights on the Torah Portion* from the Lubavitcher Rebbe.

Leshon Hara – Negative Speech

old to watch a presidential debate. Ouch. That hurts. Where have Rabbi Joshua ben Levi's wise words gone: "a person should never utter an ugly word?" We've had ugly words tossed about with such abandon that it has compromised the dignity of leadership itself.

I was struck by the contrast of this dilemma to something I saw in one of the most inspiring books I've read in years: *Rebbe: The Life and Teachings of Menachem M. Shneerson, the Most Influential Rabbi of Modern History.*

Rabbi Shneerson (1902-1994), affectionately known as the Rebbe, was the seventh and last head of Chabad-Lubavitch, a Chasidic branch with roots in Russia. He created a network of outreach institutions that literally span the globe.

Researching the Rebbe's life for five years, Rabbi Joseph Telushkin, the book's author, realized that the Rebbe went to extreme lengths to avoid the use of negative words. Rabbi Telushkin examined 40 years of the Rebbe's public lectures and concluded that the Rebbe did not criticize people by name even when he questioned a behavior. He also never used the term "beit cholim" or hospital. House of the sick, as it is literally translated, is a discouraging expression. Instead he preferred "beit refuah," a house of healing. In a letter to Professor Mordechai Shani, director of the Sheba Medical Center in Israel, he once wrote, "Even though ... this would seem to represent only a semantic change, the term "beit refuah" brings encouragement to the sick, it represents more accurately the goal of the institution ... which is to bring about a complete healing. Therefore, why call it by a word that does not suit its intentions?"

The Rebbe understood and modeled something obvious and potent, namely words have connotations and denotations. The choices we make influence the way we regard what we are talking about. That being the case, why choose to say something negatively when you can communicate the same message in an elevated fashion?

As another illustration, the Rebbe also did not like the term used by the IDF (the Israeli Defense Forces) to refer to those wounded by their war service: "nechai Tzahal," literally, army handicapped. After the 1973 Yom Kippur War, the Rebbe said, "If a person has been deprived of a limb or a faculty, this itself indicates that God has also given him special powers to overcome the limitations this entails, and to surpass the achievement of ordinary people."

Part Two

He preferred a different term that would reflect on their service rather its cost: "metzuyanim" or exceptional veterans.

In the 50s and 60s when terms like moron, retard and idiot (it hurts to write this) were still widely in use to describe the mentally disabled, the Rebbe used the word "special," decades before it became common parlance.

The Rebbe also did not like to say evil and instead said, "hefech Hatov," the opposite of good. He did not even like the term "deadline" preferring instead the due date – using a term referencing birth rather than death. You could say this is a stretch, but perhaps the Rebbe had internalized the words of Genesis one. Words create and destroy worlds, real and emotional.

He often said, "Think good, and it will be good," years before the school of positive psychology was born. To a man who complained that his children were assimilating and regularly used the Yiddish expression, "It's hard to be a Jew," the Rebbe responded, "Then that is the message your children hear and that is the impression of Judaism they have." The Rebbe challenged this father to use another Yiddish expression, "It's good to be a Jew."

All this positivity and feel-good language might be hard for the more cynical among us to stomach. Yet it's high time that we demand that politicians, celebrities and athletes stop throwing words around like bullies or hurling invectives at each other with little thought about how it shifts our general use of language. And while we're at it, maybe we can all release a little of our "inner Rebbe" and try a softer word, a more gentle tone, a more embracing and loving approach.

Today's challenge: Spend one entire day avoiding any negative speech. Shabbat is a great day to keep it holy.

Speak No Evil [86]
Chaya Shuchat [87]

Being the target of gossip can make things very awkward, very quickly. How do you act around people who've been talking about you behind your back? Do you continue to relate to them as

---

86   Based on Likutei Sichot, vol. 22, pp. 70-80.
87   www.chabad.org

Leshon Hara – Negative Speech

though nothing happened? Confront the gossiper directly? Resort to some form of passive-aggressive retaliation? Or maybe retreat from social interaction to nurse your wounds in private?

Gossip can lead to destroyed friendships, loss of self-confidence, increased stress, illness, job loss, and even suicide. But though we're viscerally aware of the negative effects of gossip, how many of us can say that we've never indulged in it ourselves? Maybe we simply want to be in the know and not miss out on "important" information. Maybe we've felt the sting of someone's nasty personality and want confirmation that we're not alone. Maybe we're projecting our own insecurities and weaknesses onto others. But constantly bathing in negativity takes its toll on us as well. We all take part in creating our environment, and whatever poison we contribute, we will have to live with its effects.

The Gemara says that *Leshon Hara* – spreading true, derogatory information about someone else – harms three people: the speaker, the listener and the subject of the gossip.[88] During Biblical times, the punishment for evil speech was swift: the speaker would be stricken with *tzaraat*, a disease that required one to be isolated from the camp.

Ever since the Holy Temple was destroyed and the Jewish people were dispersed, *tzaraat* no longer afflicts those who speak evil speech. No longer do spiritual phenomena immediately manifest themselves in physical form. But it is clear that those who engage in gossip, constant criticism and negativity also suffer a host of physical ills. The Torah's message – to avoid speaking ill of others, and to bring out their strengths through positive speech – is, unsurprisingly, also a recipe for a physically and psychologically healthy life.

So, how do we stop the epidemic of gossip? Oddly enough, dwelling at length on the negative effects of gossip does little to stop its spread. It seems that the more we talk about how terrible it is to gossip, the stronger our urge to indulge in it becomes. We condemn the gossiper while not confronting the ways that we feed into it.

This week we read the dual Torah portions of *Tazria* and *Metzora*. The portion of *Tazria* discusses the various symptoms and identifying marks of *tzaraat*, while *Metzora* deals with the purification process.

---

88 Talmud, Erachin 15b.

Part Two

The names of the two joined *parshiot*, however, could not be more different in character. The word *tazria* means "to conceive," and the *parsha* begins with the laws of a woman who has just given birth. *Metzora* refers to one who has *tzaraat*, a serious condition likened to death.[89]

Yet the juxtaposition of these two names gives us a powerful insight into overcoming the negative effects of gossip and slander. The recovery process for the *metzora* holds within it the key to *tazria* – the flourishing of new life. The enforced isolation of the *metzora* is intended as a time of self-reflection and personal growth.

When we find ourselves caught in a web of gossip, that's a clue that we need to take a break. We need to step outside that social interaction until we can figure out what's going wrong. What inner need of ours is going unfulfilled, to the point that we are taking our frustrations out on others? Are we feeling small and depleted, and trying to put down others to compensate? Or maybe we're just bored, and need more stimulating activities to occupy our mind. The way to stop *Leshon Hara* is not by condemning it, but by isolating it – reflecting on the circumstances that lead to it, and finding ways to nurture ourselves so we have less of a need to demean others.

What is true of *tzaraat* is true of all punishments mentioned in the Torah – they are not meant as retribution, but as opportunities for healing and recovery. The most extreme form of isolation found in the Torah is *galut* (exile) – banishment from our land and from God's presence. We may wonder what severe sins we could have committed to justify our lengthy exile and persecution.

But as we learn from the name *Tazria-Metzora*, the purpose of exile is not just punishment. Whatever we are going through now is meant to lead to a greater rebirth. The future revelation "is dependent on our deeds and work over the course of exile," as explained in Tanya.[90]

Whatever our circumstances are, challenging or painful as they may be, they are given to us as an opportunity to work through them and come to a place of greater insight and understanding. Then we realize that the struggles and the growth are intertwined – not that one leads to or follows the other.

---

89 Talmud, Nedarim 64b.
90 Tanya, part 1, ch. 37.

In the days of Moshiach, the complete picture will be revealed to us. We will see how every mitzvah we did during exile, every act of fortitude and courage, directly brought the redemption, on a personal and universal level.

Thought, Speech, and Action
Rabbi Ariel Sholklapper

At the end of *Parshat Emor* (Leviticus 21:1-24:23), framing the section that mirrors Hammurabi's Code of "eye for an eye, tooth for a tooth" we learn that not only could one be found liable, held accountable, and even put to death for physical actions, one could even be put to death for blasphemous speech. Speaking ill of God is a capital offense punishable by public stoning.

"And he that blasphemes the name of the Lord, he shall surely be put to death; all the congregation shall certainly stone him; as well the stranger, as the home-born, when he blasphemes the Name, shall be put to death" (24:16).

Confronting the difficulty of reigning in our speech is truly one of the most difficult requirements of our tradition and of all spiritual practice. In a recent podcast, Rabbi Bradley Artson, Dean of the Ziegler School of Rabbinic Studies, when asked what the hardest mitzvah is to uphold, responded, "I think the hardest mitzvah to observe is *Shmirat Halashon*, avoiding malicious speech, (...) because it plays into our own insecurities. We think that we can buy social acceptance by trashing someone else. In part because we put our energy into technically not violating it, while completely upending it" (March 25, 2015). And the challenge is real. It can often feel like just speaking is not harmful. That unless we actually DO something, take some action, we should not or cannot be held accountable. But, our words carry weight and power.

The Talmud, Bava Metziah 58b, notes this insight in a discussion on whether monetary or verbal affliction is a worse offense, Rabbi Shmuel son of Nahmani (3rd-4th century, Israel) says, "One can be repaid, however the other is not possible to repay." Indeed, financial loss can be recompensed, but once psychological damage is inflicted, it is infinitely more difficult to remunerate. In recent years Rabbi Shmuel son of Nahmani's insight received bonafide scientific backing.

In an article entitled "Relational Psychosis Psychotherapy: A Neuropsychoanalytic Model," Dr. Brian Koehler of NYU, writes about the extreme neurological impact verbal abuse, including bullying, takes on the psyche. He sites developmental traumatologist Martin Teicher's 2006 work which proposed that verbal abuse impacts "a cascade of physiological and neurohumoral responses…", and maintains that neurological structures and even genetic expression are adversely impacted (p. 17). The ultimate results of which includes severe psychological disorders. Verbal abuse alone can literally upend another person's life.

These psychotherapists unearthed what anybody who is still dealing with the pain resulting from the words of others is feeling. They showed that words leave deep yet invisible scars. It is not for nothing that in recent years anti-bullying initiatives have gained support in schools. The common saying "sticks and stones may break my bones, but words will never hurt me," got it wrong. Yes, we should be weary of the stones, but words certainly do hurt. Our words can do unimaginable damage and rightfully should carry heavy consequence.

Our tradition emphasizes the importance of proper speech, toward God and toward one another for a simple reason. Each person has a Divine spark within them. When speaking maliciously toward another person, we discount that Godly spark. Consequently, verbal abuse of a fellow human is a form of blaspheming God.

Rabbi Akiva (1st-2nd century, Israel) is quoted in Pirkei Avot (3:16) as imparting the now famous wisdom *"Siag la'khohmah sh'tikah"* or "The safeguard for wisdom is silence." Speak less and speak more intently; take great care to speak with kindness and not to harm others.

Rambam (1135-1204, Egypt), in the Mishneh Torah Sefer Madda Hilkhot Deot Chapter two expands on Rabbi Akiva's lesson and provides some principles to help guide our speech. He writes, "Silence is a safeguard for wisdom. Therefore, one should not hasten to answer, nor speak at length. He should teach his students in calm and tranquility without shouting or wordiness." This is what Solomon stated: "The words of the wise are heard in tranquility" (Ecclesiastes 9:17).

Leshon Hara – Negative Speech

We must take the plea of our tradition seriously; this challenge pervades our lives. How many times have we spoken ill of another, either to them or behind their back, feeling it was innocent and inconsequential? We must ask ourselves how we can do better, how can we become more aware of our speech and refrain from harmful speech. We must also pass this lesson on to our children. We must ask ourselves: How can we convey the importance of speaking with care and kindness? How do we teach them that just as there are consequences for their actions, there are consequences for their words? In order to live a praiseworthy life, we must teach ourselves and our children how to gain better self control, speech included. We must teach them "if you have nothing good to say, better not to say anything at all," "*Siag la'khohmah shtikah.*" It is better to say nothing, and to sit in uncomfortable silence, than to harm another human being.

Words That Help, Words That Heal
Rabbi Joseph Telushkin

Every year, tens of thousands of families are split asunder and close friendships are broken because contending parties refuse to fight fairly. In a dispute with someone, you have the right to state your case, express your opinion, explain why you think the other party is wrong, even make clear how passionately you feel about the subject at hand. But these are the only rights you have.

You do not have the moral right to undercut your adversary's position by invalidating him or her personally … Words have consequences, and if you use them to hurt people, your victims will find ways to hurt you in return.

The Tongue Set Free?
Rabbi David Wolpe

The most frequently cited sins in Jewish tradition are sins of speech. Some are direct, such as gossiping or slander. Others are indirect, such as embarrassing someone in public, which is usually

Part Two

a consequence of saying something callous or unkind.

As a result, *shemirat haLeshon*, guarding one's tongue, is a powerful value in Judaism. In part this is because we recognize the potency of words.

If I tell you something discreditable about another person, even if it is later disproved, I cannot force you to forget and the faint whiff of scandal sticks to their reputation, even if wholly undeserved. One of our greatest sages, the Chofetz Chaim, devoted much of his life to exploring and explaining the ins and outs of proper speech.

Why is it so hard to avoid negative speech? Because it so powerful. "He is a nice guy" does not have the punch of "He is a jerk." But Jewish tradition reminds us that loose, cruel speech is wrong, whether done privately or publicly.

I hope all around dinner tables in the Jewish world parents are explaining that whatever their political position, our sages are unanimous on the importance of dignified speech, and the destructive power of the tongue set free.

Spiritual Toxicity
Rabbi Yechiel Eckstein

Imagine someone invites you out to lunch. You sit down to a great-looking meal with a group of friends. Everything seems perfect, and you are ready for a fun time. Everyone eats and enjoys the meal. However, when you get home, you start to feel nauseous. It turns out the food was toxic. And to make matters worse, the friend who "hosted" the meal paid for it at someone else's expense.

In retrospect, that meal wasn't so great after all. In fact, you wish you had not gone.

This scenario may seem familiar, but in a different guise. This is often how we feel after sitting with friends who serve up nothing but gossip. At first, what's being offered seems juicy and enticing. But after a steady diet of gossip, we often feel sick. Everyone may have had a great time, but at someone else's expense. And irreparable damage has been done.

In fact, the Jewish sages teach that when gossip is passed along, it is as if three people die. Who are those three people?

Leshon Hara – Negative Speech

The most obvious person to be impacted is the person who is the object of the gossip. As the human being is diced and sliced and served up as fodder for a good time, reputations are destroyed. There is a reason why a term for embarrassment is "losing face." When someone is disgraced by gossip, his or her identity is destroyed; it's a kind of death. And following the destruction of that person, the by-product is often the destruction of precious relationships.

The second person considered "dead" is the speaker of the gossip. When God created humans, the distinguishing element between humans and animals was a human's ability to speak. God's intention was that people would use speech for good things, like prayer, encouragement, and other positive communication. Each time we use this ability for destruction, we betray the very purpose of God's creation. In essence, we "kill" a little bit more of the human being God created in His own image.

The third person that "dies" from gossip is the listener. Gossip is like spiritual pollution, and like secondhand smoke, it can kill.

In Proverbs we read: *"The words of a gossip are like choice morsels; they go down to the inmost parts."* Once you listen to gossip, its toxic energy is inside you. This is why we feel sick.

Let's resolve to stay away from toxic gossip. Remember, God gave us two hands to cover up our two ears when necessary! Life is too short to waste time speaking badly about other people or listening to "dirt" about others. Speak kindly and truthfully. In doing so, we will help purify the spiritual environment and create a healthier climate for everyone.

Use Your Words
Rabbi Natan Fenner[91]

Jewish tradition has a rich perspective on the power of speech. Words convey our thoughts and feelings and devotional intentions; words can be the vehicle for blessing and bestowing honor upon one another; words can be the instruments of great hurt and destruction. Contracts can be sealed or broken; relationships reinforced or betrayed; armies goaded or calmed based on the

---

91   © Bay Area Jewish Healing Center

Part Two

choice and tone of our utterances. In the Creation narrative of Genesis, the world comes into being through the agency of Divine speech. The writings of the Chofetz Chaim (the late 19th- early 20th century scholar Israel Meyer Kagan) illustrate how so much of a person's experience and reputation in the world can be damaged or destroyed through hurtful, deceitful, or slanderous speech. Talking, and refraining from talking, are among the most profound human actions.

The Torah (of *Parshat Mattot*) reading begins with the mitzvah of keeping a vow. We are instructed to "do according to all that proceeds out of (our) mouth" (Numbers 30:3) when we have sworn an oath. The act of giving our word, or invoking the name of the Divine, is meant to "bind one's soul with a bond." Making a promise to another person, to ourselves, or to God can be a way of giving ourselves the additional strength and motivation to "keep our word" and follow through, for good. The specter of breaking such a vow – knowing the personal and moral consequences – may help keep us from straying in the face of temptation or distraction. The awareness of those consequences can also keep us from making vows and promises lightly, and from setting up expectations of ourselves or others that may not be met.

Most of us can easily remember a time when we felt disappointed, even emotionally crushed, when someone else failed to keep a vow, broke a promise, shattered our expectations, or simply forgot to meet us at an appointed time. These are sobering reminders of how we need to be careful about what comes out of our mouths.

Rebbe Nahman of Bratzlav once said, "If you have the power to destroy, you also have the power to repair." Likewise we recognize that our speech can be used both to curse and to bless, to hurt and to forgive. We are instructed to choose life and blessing, in order that our lives and those around us may be filled with blessing.

In times of illness, loss, or transition, we may be especially vulnerable to the words and tone of speech of people around us, including family, friends, familiar caregivers and total strangers. We may also have less energy to articulate our own needs and desires, to give voice to our gratitude and praise, to encourage, or to channel or vent our anger in healthy and constructive ways.

If you know someone who is in a vulnerable place right now, think about how your words might touch them. What is the impact of your physical proximity, of your eye contact or your "focus" on the phone or your written words? How do you convey your empathy, your love and support, your earnest concern, or your willingness to listen and learn? How are your words and your intentions received? What do you most want to express.

If you are in a vulnerable place, you can take note of how the content and manner of your conversations affect you. You might think about what you appreciate – from the good wishes to the information-sharing to the social conversation – or what you would like to change for the better (if you have some "say" in the matter). What do you most want to hear, or say?

All of us can reflect – perhaps even aloud – on how we can use our many daily conversations as opportunities to bring more blessing and healing to one another.

How to Use Your Most Powerful Weapon
Rabbi Yael Hammerman[92]

We are defined by how we use our tongues and by the words that leave our lips each day.

Everyone is born with a powerful weapon, which can be used for both good and evil. This weapon grows over time, but remains small and mostly concealed. It's bumpy, pink and slippery, but can be pulled out and put away in a blink of an eye. This weapon is your tongue. Your tongue is used to create thousands of words every day, and each word has the power to harm or to heal, to hurt or to help. We are defined by how we use our tongues and by the words that leave our lips each day.

The Torah portion, *Tazria*, teaches us about the strength of words. The ancient Sages believed that leprosy was a punishment for slander and spreading malicious gossip. By gossiping, you hurt someone's reputation and make them appear poorly in public. In return, you are punished with a skin disease that causes you to appear poorly before others.

---

92   From Torah Topics for Today.

Part Two

Once words are released, they cannot be brought back. Your tongue is like an arrow. Once unleashed, it cannot be withdrawn. Like arrows, words have the ability to pierce those with whom they come in contact. We must be careful with our most precious weapons, our tongues, and the words they create.

Talk to your kids about how our words define us, and how words can be both helpful and harmful.

Connect to their lives:
- When have your words hurt someone else?
- How did you feel after saying something hurtful?
- When has another person's words hurt you? How did it feel?
- How can you use your words to help others?
- How will you use your most powerful weapon, your tongue?

The Toothpaste Sacrifice
Rabbanit Alissa Thomas-Newborn

Like toothpaste, derogatory speech cannot be returned to the tube.

The Leprosy Of Irresponsible Speech

I remember the first time I learned about *Leshon Hara* (derogatory speech about others that is prohibited under Jewish law). I was a little girl sitting in the synagogue we belonged to, and my Rabbi explained that once you squirt out all of the toothpaste from its tube, you cannot put it back in. He said that just like the toothpaste, the words that come out of our mouths cannot be taken back. And so, I learned the lesson that every child is taught, whether directly or indirectly: What we say matters.

In *Parshat Metzora*, we read about what I will call the "toothpaste sacrifice." During the time when the Temple stood in Jerusalem, this sacrifice was offered because a person spoke derogatory words about another and as a result contracted a spiritual malady: a skin disease called *tzaraat* (the person with *tzaraat* was known as the *metzora*). According to our Sages, God afflicted those who had engaged in *Leshon Hara*. The sacrifice to begin the healing from *tzaraat* and to atone for *Leshon Hara* looked like this: "Two live, clean birds, a cedar stick, and a strip of crimson wool, and hyssop" (Leviticus 14:4).

Rashi, the 11th-century Biblical commentator, breaks down the significance of each of these elements (Rashi on Leviticus 14:4). Drawing from the Midrash and the Gemara (our Oral Tradition), he explains that birds are sacrificed in response because they constantly twitter and chirp, creating sounds like the chatter of *Leshon Hara*. Cedar stick is used because cedar trees stand tall, symbolizing haughtiness and ego, which often fuel our judgmental and hurtful speech. The crimson wool looks like a tongue, which is the physical God-given tool through which we speak, sometimes for good and sometimes for bad. And the unassuming hyssop plant represents the need for humility in the elimination of haughtiness.

With this explanation, we see our "toothpaste sacrifice" transform from a distant practice of the past to relatable advice for the present. We may not be able to put the toothpaste back into the tube and take back the destructive things we have said, but God has given us a path to a different form of healing and repair. It is key that this Divine path is not external but instead profoundly internal. An apology, though necessary, is not sufficient.

The person who has spoken *Leshon Hara* and now has *tzaraat* must also separate from the chirping and chatter – the outside influences that drown out goodness and amplify dissonance. He or she must identify the haughtiness and ego within, the proverbial cedar tree inside each of us. And then the person must do the hard work of cultivating humility. This means humility between humans and God, as illustrated in the appreciation that the tongue ultimately belongs to God and should be used in Godly ways. And this also means humility between people, as we each strive to treat each other with the humbleness and flexibility of the hyssop.

Gossip Is Not Harmless

Louis Brandeis and his law partner Samuel Warren laid out some of those reasons in a famous law review article in 1890. "Each crop of unseemly gossip," they wrote, "becomes the seed of more, and … results in the lowering of social standards and of morality. Even gossip apparently harmless, when widely and

Part Two

persistently circulated, is potent for evil. It both belittles and perverts ... inverting the relative importance of things, thus dwarfing the thoughts and aspirations of a people."

When Words Hurt
Rabbi Kerrith Solomon[93]

Our words can be used to hurt others, and in doing so we also harm ourselves. When people gossip, people get hurt. Certainly the person gossiped about is hurt, but the person listening and the person doing the gossiping are also damaged. But our words can also be used for good, to help build people up instead of to break them down.

In this week's Torah portion, Miriam is punished for speaking ill of her brother Moses. While we might not break into boils when we gossip or spread rumors, it certainly can make us ugly on the inside.

There is a story that is often told about the dangers of gossip. One version tells that a woman spreads untruths about a neighbor in her village. When she wants to make amends, she approaches an elder in the community, tells him how sorry she is, and asks what she can do to apologize. He brings her to the top of a hill on a windy day with a pillowcase full of feathers. He instructs her to open the pillowcase, and the feathers fly everywhere. He then asks her to collect the far-flung feathers. She protests, saying that it is impossible to track down each feather. He responds that so too is it impossible to undo the damage that gossip causes, for each piece of gossip told catches the wind and travels far, just like the feathers.

Talk to your kids about where they have seen or experienced gossip.

Connect to their lives:

- Have you ever participated in spreading gossip?
- What effect did it have on the person it was about?

---

93   From *Values and Ethics: Torah Topics for Today,* © Behrman House, Inc., included with permission www.behrmanhouse.com.

- What effect did it have on you?
- What would you do differently if you had the chance?

Electronic Leshon Hara
Sinful Words from Sinful People
Rabbi Marc D. Angel

Years ago, I – along with many others – regularly received envelopes stuffed with pages put together by a group that claimed to represent "authentic" Judaism. The authors believed themselves to be the sole arbiters of true Judaism, and they vilified those who deviated from their views. Their screeds were drenched in hateful, slanderous language ... and it seems not to have occurred to them that *Leshon Hara* – evil gossip – is a highly serious sin.

Halakha teaches that just as it is forbidden to communicate *Leshon Hara*, so it is a transgression to receive it. I sent the authors several requests to remove me from their mailing list, but they ignored my requests. I finally came up with a great idea. The next time I received one of their mailings, I took a red magic marker and wrote in large letters on the front of the envelope: RETURN TO SENDER: OBSCENE MATERIAL. That solved the problem. I received no more mail from them.

When such people engage in gossip/slander/defamation of character, they are indeed generating obscene material. They somehow delude themselves into thinking that they alone are God's policemen and that they are permitted to defame people whose views they deem not sufficiently religious. Their misguided and self-righteous behavior reflects an incredible religious arrogance ... and sinfulness.

The problem has become far more severe now that people can spread their defamations via electronic means. They reach thousands of readers by posting their venom on websites, or entering malicious material on Wikipedia, or sending emails.

Rambam points out that among the sins for which there is almost no possible atonement is the sin of maligning someone in public. Even if one eventually wishes to repent, he/she will not know who heard the sinful words and therefore cannot ever be sure he/she can reach everyone to retract the wicked statements. Evil words, once made public, are impossible to retract fully. All the more so with "electronic *Leshon Hara*."

Modern technology makes it quite easy for people to post hostile remarks against those with whom they disagree. These ad hominem attacks gain lives of their own, being forwarded to readers who then forward them to others, etc. People feel that it's fine for them to vent, to call names, to discredit others. In their self-righteousness, they don't realize the gravity of their transgressions.

The Talmud teaches that the ancient Temple in Jerusalem was destroyed because of *sinat hinam*, gratuitous hatred. A key feature of *sinat hinam* is the use of derogatory language.

In a fascinating responsum,[94] Rabbi Naftali Tsvi Yehudah Berlin – the Netsiv – reminded his readers that during the time of the Second Temple, the Jewish people were divided between the Perushim and Tsedukim. Competition between the groups was intense. The situation became so bad that Perushim branded as a Tseduki anyone who deviated even slightly from prevailing practice. To dissent from the predominant opinion led to one's being ostracized. The Netsiv applied the lesson to his own time: "It is not difficult to imagine reaching this situation in our time, Heaven forbid, that if one of the faithful thinks that a certain person does not follow his way in the service of God, then he will judge him as a heretic. He will distance himself from him. People will pursue one another with seeming justification (*beHeter dimyon*), Heaven forbid, and the people of God will be destroyed, Heaven forfend."

When people – including those who think of themselves as being religious – spread defamatory material, they undermine the moral fabric of society. They do not teach "truth," but rather become models of what religious people should not be. They desecrate the Torah they claim to defend and honor.

In an age of mass communication, the dangers of *sinat hinam* and *Leshon Hara* are greatly exacerbated. Here is some basic advice on how to cope with this serious problem.

1. Do not post ad hominem attacks or engage in character assassination. If you object to someone's opinions, then focus on

---

94   Meshiv Davar, no. 44.

the opinions. Offer cogent arguments. Be respectful.

2. If you receive a comment/blog/email that contains *Leshon Hara*, delete it immediately. Do not forward it to anyone else. If possible, communicate with the sender and register your disapproval of his/her spreading of *Leshon Hara*.

3. Do not trust the credibility of those who engage in defamation/*Leshon Hara*. If they have no compunctions about defaming others, they'll have no compunction about defaming you!

Remember that our Temple was destroyed because of *sinat hinam* and *Leshon Hara*. Those who engage in these sins are committing a terrible injustice not just to their victims, but to our entire community and society. When they pose as being upholders of authentic Orthodoxy, their sins are particularly reprehensible. How will they ever be able to repent? Will they even realize that they need to repent?

The daily *Amidah* prayer has a concluding meditation: "Oh Lord, guard my tongue from evil and my lips from speaking deceitfully." Let everyone pay close attention to these words and strive to live up to them. To pray them and not mean them makes a mockery of the prayer ... and a mockery of one's own purported religiosity. *Leshon Hara* is obscene material. It must be avoided, it must be rejected, it must be returned to sender for atonement.

Your Word Is Your Bond
Rabbi Yisroel Jungreis

Moshe commands the leaders of the tribes, and through them, the entire nation, regarding the sanctity of vows and the tragic consequences of not keeping one's word, which the Torah regards as a desecration.

Our entire faith is linked to the sanctity of speech. It is through speech that we committed ourselves to an eternal covenant with Hashem when we proclaimed "*Naaseh v'nishma.*"

It is through speech, via prayer and Torah study that we continue to connect with our Hashem.

It is through speech that we give expression to the Divine spark that Hashem breathed into our beings.

Part Two

It is through speech that Hashem created the world.

It is through speech that we, in our own human fashion, send forth positive or negative energies.

As stated previously, death and life are in the hands of the tongue.

To protect us from using our tongues irresponsibly, Hashem places them behind two gates, our teeth and our lips, so that before we speak, we may weigh and measure our words, for once they are spoken, we cannot easily undo them or take them back.

The damage wrought by broken promises, curses, and painful or blasphemous words cannot be easily erased.

The converse, of course, is also true.

Kind, warm, loving words are balm for the soul and have the power to transform darkness into light and despair into hope. "*Chaim Biyad HaLeshon*" – life is in the hands of the tongue.

Creating Your World Through Language
Rabbi Dianne Cohler-Esses[95]

Just as the world was created through language in Genesis, we all create our personal worlds every day through speech. We can both create and destroy with words. We can hurt other people through speaking negatively about them. Speaking about people behind their back, we can harm reputations, and thereby even harm friendships and business. Reputation in our very social and interdependent world is at the heart of one's status both personally and professionally.

Jewish tradition is particularly sensitive to the power of speech and how it can be damaging. Our Torah portion this week addresses the consequences caused by speaking negatively about others, an act that is called *Leshon Hara* or Evil Talk. It includes slander, gossip, and other kinds of destructive language.

The first place to practice not engaging in Evil Talk is in the family. Think for a moment: how do siblings talk about one another? How does the family engage in talking about neighbors?

---

95 Joyce and Fred Claar, *Values and Ethics: Torah Topics for Today*, Behrman House Publishers.

Leshon Hara – Negative Speech

Within our families we may see this kind of speech as internal and therefore harmless. However, how families speak about one another creates a model for how children will speak outside of the home about their friends. The less parents permit and model this kind of negative speech, the less likely children will use it on their own.

Talk to your kids about the Jewish prohibition of *Leshon Hara* or Evil Talk and explain the negative consequences of this behavior.

Connect to their lives:
- Why do you think it might be important not to say negative things about others?
- How do you feel when you find out someone has said something negative about you?
- Why do you think people like to gossip and find it so appealing?
- What might help you to engage in it less?

Part Three

Misusing Speech

Part Three

Strictly, Major, Extremely: How Words Lose their Meaning
Rabbi Marc D. Angel

Some words get overused, misused and abused. The words become degraded so that they no longer can be taken at face value.

The word "kosher" is an example of a word that has become compromised. The packaging on kosher foods reflects the problem. The word "kosher," by itself, seems no longer to indicate that a product is actually kosher. Much packaging states that the product is under "strict Rabbinic supervision," or that it is "strictly kosher;" apparently, without the words "strict" or "strictly" we couldn't trust its *kashruth*. Some packaging now states that the product is under the "strictest Rabbinic supervision," implying that just being "strict" or "strictly kosher" isn't kosher enough. Only "strictest" should be trusted.

To complicate matters, we often find products that are under multiple Rabbinic supervisions ... as many as four or five different *hashgahot* per item. Does having multiple *hashgahot* make the product more kosher? Are those items with only one or even two *hashgahot* not kosher enough?

The word "kosher" has been degraded; many people apparently don't trust the word unless it is accompanied by "strict," "strictly" or "strictest;" or unless it is authenticated by multiple *hashgahot*. This may be the fault of manufacturers, or of *kashruth* agencies, or of consumers ... but the result is to downgrade the word "kosher" and to confuse the public.

The word "major" is another example of a compromised word.

We receive notices from various congregations and organizations announcing lectures, *shiurim*, and a variety of programs. Apparently, it is felt that just announcing the topic is inadequate to gain people's attention. So we are told that the upcoming lecture/*shiur*/program is "important." But since everything seems to be "important" these days, the announcements inform us that the upcoming event is "special." Recently, I've begun receiving notices for upcoming lectures/*shiurim* that are "major." But if these lectures/*shiurim* are "major," does that imply that they are more significant than if they were just "special" or "important?" And does that imply that all "non-major" lectures, *shiurim*/programs are "minor?" When hyping events as "major," the result is to downgrade all other "non-major" events ... and ultimately to downgrade "major" itself.

Another phrase that has been popping up is "extremely brilliant." It seems that just being smart, intelligent or even brilliant is no longer enough; one needs to be "extremely brilliant." Yet, if so many people are upgraded to being "extremely brilliant," then the phrase loses its significance. If you really want to stand out, you'll need to find a phrase that goes higher than "extremely brilliant." But then, many others will adopt that new phrase too, in a never-ending effort to outdo others. The more hyperbole we use, the less the words really mean.

Wouldn't it be nice if people used words carefully, without need for hyperbole? It would be a very strictly, major, and extremely brilliant thing to do!

Words, Just Words
Rabbi Michael Rascoe

Twenty times over the course of Yom Kippur, we confess our sins via the *Ashamnu* and the *Al Het*. In these two confessions, we recite 68 specific sins, yet not one of them concerns ritual. For example, we don't mention desecrating Sabbaths or Festivals, or the eating of *treif,* non-kosher foods. In fact we don't mention any sin solely between God and us. We only detail sins between people, since any sin against another person is also a transgression against God.

Merely saying a list of sins, however, does not effect atonement. The *Vidui*, confession, is not a literary device. "The prerequisites of ("repentance," of) God's forgiveness" for sins against other people, "are reparation, restitution, and reconciliation with the person who has been wronged." Sometimes, therefore, God's full forgiveness is impossible to obtain, such as in the case of a person who directs abusive language at a group of people and who cannot apologize to every single individual, or in the case of a person who appropriates what belongs to the poor and underprivileged and who cannot locate the homeless person affected, in order to apologize.

Part Three

If we look more carefully at the enumerated transgressions, we notice they're not abstracts or remote categorizations. They instead reflect the varieties of sin that lead us from occasional lapses of judgment into "persistent vice." The sins listed are "the stuff of daily life, and point an accusing finger at our repeated moral failures." We express contrition for attitudes, such as pride, callousness, insolence and envy; for deeds, such as the pursuit of unlawful gain, corrupt business practices, and deception; and for the deficiencies of our spirit, such as the energetic pursuit of evil and the deterioration of respect for authority, especially for parents and teachers. [1]

But if we look real closely at the list, we realize that 1/4 of the specific sins are about the abuse of our capacities of speech, such as slander, gossip, lying, offensive speech, evil advice, insincerity, and idle speech. All 16 or so sins of our mouth are different. As a colleague of mine once said, "I believe if a Jew did nothing else on Yom Kippur but ... determine to improve in that one area of sin, then that Jew would bring great salvation into the life of his or her dear ones and to the community."

The spoken word can "build or destroy human relationships." "They can gladden a heart or bring a human being low."[2]

Dr. Bernard Lown, the renowned Boston cardiologist, tells two stories of the power of words. In one case, a middle-aged librarian had a narrowing of the tricuspid valve on the right side of her heart. Though occasionally causing her problems, she had lived with it for years. One day, while in the hospital, the chief cardiologist, who had been treating her for ten years, greeted her warmly, and said to his retinue, "this woman has TS" and he left. Immediately, she became frightened and began to hyperventilate. When Dr. Lown asked her why she became upset, she replied that TS stood for "terminal situation." Dr. Lown tried to explain to her that TS actually meant "tricuspid stenosis" and she had been living with it for years and would continue to do so. He then tried to find the doctor in order to reassure her, but he couldn't and she died that same day.

Dr. Lown's second story concerns a seemingly hopeless heart attack victim under oxygen who presumably was unaware of his

---
1   Arzt, Justice and Mercy, pp. 195-6, 216-8.
2   Potok, Ethical Living, pp. 174, 177.

surroundings. During rounds, Dr. Lown told the staff that the patient "had a wholesome, very loud third-sound gallop." What this means is that the heart muscle is straining and usually failing. Yet the patient suddenly began improving and eventually was discharged from the hospital. During a checkup some months later, when asked about his miraculous improvement, the patient said, "Doctor ... I was sure the end was near and that you and your staff had given up hope. However, Thursday morning, when you entered with your troops ... you listened to my heart; you seemed pleased by the findings and announced ... that I had a wholesome gallop. I knew that doctors, in talking to me, might try to soften things. But I knew they wouldn't kid each other. So ... I figured I still had a lot of kick to my heart and could not be dying. My spirits were for the first time lifted, and I knew I would live and recover."

As the Book of Proverbs (18:21) so aptly puts it, "Life and death are in the power of the tongue." The power of words does affect us. If you say to your spouse, "You look beautiful," s/he feels good all day. If you instead say to your spouse, after the breakfast is ruined again, "You always ruin it. Can't you do anything right?" the day, too, is ruined.

It's no accident that husbands who kiss their wives good-bye in the morning have fewer collisions on their way to work than husbands who don't talk to their wives in the morning. If you say to a child, "I'm sure you can do it," you bolster his/her esteem and the child will succeed in life. But if you tell a child "Go ahead, but don't expect to succeed," you discourage and dispirit him/her and you will create a timid, repressed and unsuccessful life. "Life and death are in the power of the tongue."

The power of misused words so concerned the Rabbis, they claimed that slanderers deny God and that God and a slanderer cannot inhabit the world at the same time. Indeed, the sages say, the scoffer, the liar, the flatterer, and the spreader of malicious gossip cannot receive the Divine Presence[3] and whoever tells tales about someone in secret has no portion in the world to come.[4] One Rabbi even went so far as to say, "There is no atonement for defaming an individual."[5]

Slander, for the Rabbis, is worse than bloodshed, incest or

---

3   All Bavli Arakhin 15b.
4   Pirqei DeRabbi Eliezer, 53.
5   Yerushalmi, Bava Qama 8:10.

idolatry.[6] It is more destructive than murder, for one who commits murder kills only one person, while a slanderer kills three – himself, the listener, and the victim.[7] To use the Rabbis' metaphor, slander is more difficult to endure than the sword.[8] A sword kills once, while slander can kill again and again, very slowly. A sword wound can be healed; a slander never disappears.

The Rabbis graphically and deliberately used extremely harsh language for good reason. As the Talmud says, a number of people commit robbery, a small number commit incest, but almost everybody causes someone else to slander.[9] Slander is as vicious as the Rabbis claim. The first slanted story works precisely because no one knows it's slander, so we slander again and again. We've all seen it in the business world, or in organizational work as someone climbs to the top. As Steve Strasser in his business column has observed on numerous occasions, it's tempting but immoral. And he continues that one rises only so far by gossip because it destroys your competition without enhancing you. In addition, he adds, eventually it comes back to haunt you either because the truth eventually turns up or because someone else will slander you in an environment that rewards it.

We slander for two reasons that are really the flip side of one coin. To get ahead, we slander in order to boost our own ego, when we actually feel inferior. Or, we slander in order to protect our post because we think we're better than the others and they shouldn't be allowed to get in our way, so we tear them down. In either case, our ego is at work. As I said on Rosh HaShanah, quoting the Zlotzover Maggid, our ego and our own importance stand like a wall between God and us. No relationship can exist if it's just me. Not even God can get through that barrier.

Yes, we cut out our competition, however eventually we're replaced. But did we learn from it? If we slandered and became accustomed to it, we at some point had to deal with ourselves. Usually, a slanderer rationalizes the slander away. We say everyone does it. We blame others – our environment, our circumstances, our upbringing, our spouse, our co-worker, etc. By doing this, we

---

6   Tanhuma, Metzora.
7   Midrash Tehillim 52.
8   Aggadat Bereshit 3.
9   Bavli Bava Batra 165b.

seemingly feel better because now we're victims. But all we've done is to escape from our own guilt by refusing to admit we're responsible for our actions. Our alibis, our circumlocutions, our justifications may work, but they do so at the expense of our ability to act, and at the loss of our integrity. It is hypocritical to expound ethics and abilities when our proclamations and actions are inconsistent. And while we don't notice the hypocrisy, others do.

Ann Landers describes slanderers in slightly different terms. "People with great minds talk about ideas. People with average minds talk about events. People with small minds talk about other people." When we add together the pettiness, the poor relationships, the hypocrisy, and the ego with the wish to move ahead, the Rabbis' harsh and graphic words were not so overstated.

The Rabbis were so concerned with the problem of slander, that our English usage of the word fails to convey the many Hebrew nuances. For the Rabbis, a person can tell the truth and still slander. The Hebrew term *Leshon Hara* or the Yiddish *loshen hore,* "does not mean telling lies about someone. Telling an out-and-out lie is another kind of transgression. *Leshon Hara* is when we say something true about a person with intent to hurt the person.

But *Leshon Hara* has other meanings as well. Too much flattery or praising someone amidst people who don't care for him/her are also examples of *Leshon Hara*. In fact, these two examples are even worse, for the speaker causes the listener to retort and thereby unwittingly utter *Leshon Hara*. In the Talmud's words, "Do not praise an acquaintance too highly lest others who hear will say, 'Why do you praise him/her, didn't s/he do such and such?'"[10] Both people, the speaker and the retorter, according to the Talmud, are guilty of *Leshon Hara*. In many ways, a slanderer in English is closer to the *rakhil*, the gossipmonger in Hebrew, who goes from person to person saying, "A said such-and-such about B."

Foul language, lying, tale-bearing in secret, telling the truth about someone with intent to do harm, and provoking others to utter hurtful truths are all instances of the destructive power of words.

The Rabbis were so concerned about the ruinous effects of misused language that they offered specific suggestions to help

---

10   Bava Batra 165b.

Part Three

us avoid it. One is to discipline ourselves to speak little, watch our words, not overly complain or praise, and stress silence. We should be civil and polite; watch what we say and give our entire attention to what the other person is saying before we even think of a response. A second way is to avoid participating in or listening to misused language. But even this way potentially leads to *Leshon Hara*. We must make it clear that we do not want to participate in *Leshon Hara*. By participating in it, we encourage it.

But we must be careful how we object to *Leshon Hara*. If we were to say, for example, "Do not speak of him; I want to know nothing about him; I do not want to tell what happened," such statements infer that the reason for not listening is not to avoid sins of our mouths but to imply that the person has done something bad that we don't want to talk about – and that is still slander.[11]

A third way to avoid slander is to study Torah. Torah can sensitize us to the effects of language and educate us in civility. Since gossip is often a by-product of idleness, study can help to prevent it. To borrow two modern sayings, garbage in – garbage out; impure in – impure out.

What we feed our brains conditions what comes out of our mouths. The child's game of telephone can illustrate this point. In Ann Landers' version, Mrs. A. visits Mrs. B. and mentions that she and Mr. A. are taking a vacation to Hawaii in order to spend time with each other and not their careers. When Mrs. A. leaves, Mrs. B. calls Mrs. C. and tells her the A's are having problems and that Mrs. A. is going to someplace with an H – Holland. Mrs. C. tells Mrs. D. that the A's are divorcing and Mrs. A. is moving to Hong Kong. Mrs. D. tells Mrs. E. that the business is bad so Mrs. A. is leaving Mr. A. to live in Havana. And so the story continues until Mrs. Q. calls Mrs. A. and repeats her version. To which Mrs. A. responds, "Well it appears that the women in this town have taken me around the world when all I did was cross the street." Or as the Rabbis would say in four Aramaic words, "What is spoken in Rome kills in Syria."[12]

According to the Talmud, King David listened to Ziba's slander of Saul's son Mephiboshet in awarding all of Mephiboshet's lands to Ziba. But when Mephiboshet proved the slander, David only

---

11 Mishneh Torah, De'ot 7:4.
12 Bereishit Rabbah 98:19.

Misusing Speech

took away half the land from Ziba to give back to Mephiboshet.⁽¹³⁾ Consequently, the Rabbis observed that the kingdom was subsequently divided by King Solomon's sons in a tit-for-tat measure when house went against house.

So let's all be careful with our speech. Rabbi Abraham Joshua Heschel once said that we should speak like we're writing a check. Each extra zero makes a big difference, doesn't it? Words, just words!

---

13   Shabbat 56a-b.

Part Four

The Sound Of Silence

Part Four

The Eloquence Of Silence
Rabbi Abraham Joshua Heschel [1]

Job had many successors. The Kotzker[2] was one of them. His mind did not, however, follow traditional ways of asking Job's questions. The Kotzker never imitated or repeated. In his eyes all imitation was forgery, all repetition spurious. To challenge God's judgment or His failure to exercise judgment without restraint would have been foolhardy. The Kotzker reasoned with audacity but walked in awe.

Job was provoked by suffering, by apparent injustice; the Kotzker by falsehood, by lies. To him untruth was the cardinal evil, not suffering. He interpreted "Even the darkness is not dark to Thee" (Psalms 139:12) to mean: knowing that darkness comes from Thee, even the darkness is not dark. But one thing remained dark without redeeming comfort: falsehood.

We find that the Holy One, blessed be He, created everything in His world, only this stuff of falsehood He did not create, did not fashion. Out of their own hearts did mortals conceive false words, as it is said: "They conceived and uttered from the heart lying words" (Isaiah 59:13).

So we read in a medieval Hebrew work. "Many are the pangs of the wicked" (Psalms 32:10) – the evildoer is in great pain; he is full of complaints and nothing is to his liking. "But he who trusts in the Lord, mercy encompasses him."

Said Reb Mendl: He who trusts in the Lord sees everything around him as a great mercy. "Those who seek the Lord lack no good thing" (Psalms 34:11). Why? Because they see each of God's deeds as for the good.

Suffering can be accepted then. Falsehood, however, cannot.

For generations people had answered Job's terrifying question by saying that all of God's deeds are just, though His ways cannot always be comprehended. One must trust in the Lord.

---

1   Abraham Joshua Heschel (1907-1972) was a Polish-born American Rabbi and one of the leading Jewish theologians and Jewish philosophers of the 20th century. He was a professor of Jewish mysticism at the Jewish Theological Seminary of America.

2   Menachem Mendel Morgensztern of Kotzk, better known as the Kotzker Rebbe (1787-1859) was a Hasidic Rabbi and leader.

The Sound Of Silence

The liturgical poems recited on New Year's Day say that His justice is hidden, we do not see it. Reb Mendl maintained in faith that "the ordinances of the Lord are true, are righteous altogether" (Psalms 19:10). Though in this world it might seem at times that God's ways were unjust, ultimately all His ways would be revealed as just.

A Jew is called "Yehudi" after Judah, about whom Leah, his mother, said, "This time will I praise the Lord." Rashi commented, "I have reason to praise, for I have taken more than my share." Indeed, every Jew should know that whatever the Almighty does for him is more than he deserves. According to this view, then, there are no grounds for complaint against God.

The Kotzker certainly never thought of measuring devotion in terms of reward and punishment.

Even if a reversal were to occur in the Divine order, whereby I would be punished for observing a Divine commandment and rewarded for transgression, even so I would not swerve from my path and would serve God as before.

These were the words of a Kotzker Hasid, Reb Avrom of Porisov. I have already mentioned that Reb Mendl was most troubled by the problem of why God had buried Truth *before* creating man. The whole world trembled when God proclaimed, "You shall not swear *falsely* by the name of the Lord your God" (Exodus 20:7). How, then, could He have cast Truth into the ground?

This was a terrifying question, especially since men were allowed to dance upon the grave of Truth. Why did man accept the diabolical role of dancing in preventing Truth from being resurrected?

There was yet another difference between Job and the Rebbe of Kotzk. Whereas Job thought aloud, Reb Mendl's thoughts mostly remained in his heart. He was a man of few words, realizing that man could make a fool of himself by questioning, challenging, or criticizing the Creator. The phrases that a man thrust against Heaven could easily boomerang.

In his wisdom and awe, Reb Mendl knew full well how the most fiery accusations could sound like gibberish when articulated.

One of the Kotzker's disciples said, "To think a thought is easy but to express it is no mean feat. That is why we pray: 'Open the mouths of those who put their trust in Thee.'" In Kotzk they cultivated the eloquence of silence.

Part Four

Reb Mendl Yorker, another disciple, kept silent for several hours at a time surrounded by the Hasidim. Complete stillness. They sat in dread and awe. One could hear a fly crawling along the wall. After the concluding grace, one of the leading Hasidim exclaimed: "That was some gathering! He took me to task and pumped me with questions, but I held my own. I answered every single question he put to me."

The less spoken, the better. It is better to put off uttering a word, even a syllable, as long as possible. *Vayelekh Haranah* – Jacob left Beersheba and went "toward Haran" (Genesis 28:10).

Rashi commented that whenever the Hebrew preposition *lamed* is called for to denote "to" or "toward" a certain place, the Torah prefers to place the letter *hay* at the end of the word (as in *haranah*): this has the same meaning as the letter *lamed* preceding. Reb Mendl asked what advantage there was in using the letter *hay* at the end instead of *lamed* at the beginning of the word? It teaches us to restrain our speech; and to delay articulating a syllable, even for a second, is worthwhile.

A lock ought to hang over one's mouth. He who reveals what he knows has little to say. "Let your heart burst before uttering so much as a moan."

"When a man has reason to scream, and cannot though he wants to – he has achieved the greatest scream." This was Reb Mendl's interpretation of the Talmudic passage "If one enters [a house] to visit a sick person [on the Sabbath], he should say, 'It is the Sabbath, when one must not cry out, and recovery will soon come.'"

In Kotzk one did not cry. Even when in pain, one did not weep. "Silence," the Kotzker said, "is the greatest cry in the world."

"When she opened it, she saw the child, and lo, the boy was crying. She took pity on him and said: 'This is one of the Hebrew children'" (Exodus 2:6). When Pharaoh's daughter opened the basket, she was amazed. The Scripture says she saw rather than heard the child weeping. Then she said, "This must be a Hebrew child, because only a Hebrew child could weep so softly."

Job's mistake consisted in his crying out when in pain but keeping silent when all went well. Real questioning should occur in both cases. Why are things so good for me, as well as why are they so bad?

Mankind may be compared to chains that shackle the hands of

God. Job's outcry today ought to be to free God from our chains.
A teaching of the Baal Shem Tov:

> *The Romans had issued an edict forbidding Torah study. When Rabbi Akiba, one of the great masters of the Talmud, defiantly continued to teach, he was imprisoned and then tortured to death by having his flesh torn from his body with "iron combs." He bore his suffering with fortitude, welcoming his martyrdom as a unique opportunity of fulfilling the precept, "You shall love the Lord thy God with all thy heart and with all thy soul ... even if you must pay for it with your life."*
>
> *"All my days I have been troubled by this verse 'with all your soul' – namely, even if He took my soul. I said, 'When shall I have the opportunity of fulfilling this? Now that I have the opportunity shall I not fulfill it?'"*
>
> *He stretched out the word ehad ("One" in "Hear, O Israel, the Lord is our God, the Lord is One") so that he was still saying it when he expired.*
>
> *When the Holy One, blessed be He, was asked by Moses, "Is this your reward for the study of Torah?" God replied, "Silence! Thus it has risen in Thought" (meaning "such is My decree").*

What was the meaning of this answer? The Baal Shem continued:

> *The answer is ambiguous. Its true meaning is: Silence! Thus he has risen in Thought. There is a spiritual realm to which one can only rise (or attain) through martyrdom. The Almighty loved Rabbi Akiba deeply and wished to uplift him to this realm of Thought, where there was an answer to every question.*

Knowing When To Remain Silent
Rabbi Avi Weiss

What should our attitude be to our children if they commit wrongful acts?

Our *parsha* offers a response. Reuven, Ya'akov's (Jacob) eldest son, committed a heinous sin. According to the literal text, he slept with Bilhah, his father's wife (Genesis 35:22).

Ya'akov is so outraged that the sentence describing his response is left incomplete – one of the few times this occurs in the Torah. All the text says is "*vayishmah Yisrael*, – and Yisrael (Jacob) heard."

Benno Ya'akov, the German Jewish commentator, has noted that whenever the text uses the verb *shma*, to hear, without specifying what one hears, it indicates to hear but not to listen – in other words, rejection. How much more so in this verse where the sentence doesn't even end, illustrating that Ya'akov was incensed beyond description. No words could adequately express his feelings of outrage.

Yet another observation: notwithstanding Ya'akov's disgust, he remains silent.

Note that in the next sentence the Torah states Ya'akov had twelve children, the first being Reuven (Genesis 35:23,24). Why the need to mention this obvious fact?

Perhaps to underscore that had Ya'akov verbally expressed his revulsion, Reuven may have opted out, leaving Ya'akov with eleven sons. Because Ya'akov held back – not saying a word – Reuven remained in the fold, the first of the twelve.

Ya'akov's approach teaches us something about speech. On the one hand it is speech which makes us unique. Rabbi Yehuda Halevy in his Kuzari labels the human being as a *medaber*. Speaking is central to human relationships.

There are occasions, however, when it is best not to speak, as saying something could destroy a relationship. It takes great wisdom to know when it is best not to talk, not to reveal a deep hurt.

It may be that Ya'akov does not immediately speak, fearful that whatever he would say could forever sever his relationship with his eldest son. Only years later, when the relationship was solid, when Ya'akov was calmer, did he tell Reuven he had forfeited the birthright for having had relations with Bilhah (Genesis 49:4).

The test of a relationship is one's ability to take off masks, open up and express one's deepest feelings. But there are occasions when one must hold back and not speak; silence should prevail.

At times, silence is the pathway to saving a relationship.

The Sound Of Silence
Rabbi Michael Gold

"Then Moses said to Aaron, This is what the Lord meant when He said, Through those near to Me I show Myself holy, and gain glory before all the people. And Aaron was silent."
Leviticus 10:3

In this week's portion, *Parshat Shemini*, tragedy hits Aaron and his family. On the eighth day of their formal inauguration into the priesthood, his two oldest sons Nadab and Abihu bring a strange fire before the Lord. A fire comes forth from the Lord and consumes the two young men. Moses tries to bring some words of comfort, how this fire shows how close the two men were to God. But Aaron reacts with silence.

The book of Ecclesiastes teaches, "there is a time to be silent and a time to speak" (Ecclesiastes 3:7). Often like Moses, we fill the world with words when silence is a much better option. How often do people confront those who have had a loss with empty bromides:

"God does not give you anything you cannot handle."
"He is in a better place."
"God must have really wanted her."
"God must have His purpose."

The best reaction to these words is that of Aaron – silence.

In the Bible, when Job goes through his suffering, his three friends come to comfort him. For seven days they simply sit next to him, without speaking a word. Only after Job speaks do the friends respond. From this Jews learn one of the laws of visiting mourners in a house of *shiva* (the seven days of mourning). One simply comes in without saying a word. Let the mourner speak first. After the mourner speaks, we can find the appropriate response. The truth is, there are no words. Your presence in the *shiva* home says it all.

When I was called down by the Broward Sheriff's Office to the hospital the afternoon of the horrible shootings at Stoneman Douglas High School, I asked the head chaplain what I should do. He answered, simply "be there." Let people sense your presence. I was with families who lost their children that day, and other

Part Four

families whose children were in surgery. I like to hope that simply being a presence was helpful. Silence says more than filling space with words.

Does speech have a place? Ecclesiastes says there is a time to be silent and a time speak. I have sat with people months after the loss, who have asked me, "Rabbi, why did this happen to me? Is my loved one in heaven? Does the soul survive death?" These questions also come up regularly in classes that I teach. This is the appropriate time to make sense of questions of life and death. I do not claim to have all the answers. But I do believe that we are more than our bodies. When our bodies die, there is a part of us that continues to exist, at least in some spiritual dimension. Can I prove it? No. But I have a deep religious sense that it is true, that somehow the soul survives.

An adult education class, a sermon, an article or book is the appropriate time or place to discuss these issues. A person who has just had a loss, at a funeral or *shiva* house, a person does not need words. They need our presence. There is a time to be silent and a time to speak. Wisdom is knowing when each is appropriate. In our portion, Moses confronts the grieving Aaron with words about God. Aaron can only be silent.

In 1964, Simon and Garfunkel recorded one of the great songs of the sixties, "The Sound of Silence". Silence often says as much as words. There is a Hasidic tradition that says that the only words God spoke at Mt. Sinai was the first letter of the Ten Commandments, the silent *alef.* God, at the most dramatic moment in history, was silent. Yet that silence changed the course of history. Once someone asked the Tzartkover Rebbe why he had not preached for a long time. He answered that there are seventy ways to teach Torah, one of them is silence. May we all learn to communicate through the sounds of silence.

The Path Of Silence And The Path Of Words
Rabbi Yoel Glick

"In silence one can contemplate the greatness of God and bind oneself to God more than one can bind oneself through speech."

The Baal Shem Tov

There is a spiritual path of silence. It is a path that has tremendous power. Silence leads us to God consciousness.

Silence is central to meditation. It is only by learning to quiet the mind and discover the place of inner silence that our meditation will become potent and alive.

Words also have great spiritual potency. The Baal Shem teaches that when we speak words for the sake of Heaven, we arouse the "Divine utterances" by which the world was created and cause them to emanate of their spiritual livingness to the lower worlds.

The path of silence and the path of words both have many different dimensions. In exploring these two paths, we will discover how each can bring us closer to God, closer to each other, and closer to ourselves.

Words bridge the gap between people, enabling them to understand and communicate with each other. They allow our thoughts to become externalized and concretized so that others can hear, absorb and analyze them.

Silence is a means of direct soul-to-soul contact that transcends the misunderstandings and arguments that arise out of verbal communication. As Sri Ramana Maharshi explains: "From silence came thought, from thought the ego, and from ego speech. So, if speech is effective, how much more so must be its source?" [3]

Speech turns us outward and pours all our energies into our words. Speech focuses our mind on the person we are talking to, so much so that we can lose all sense of our surroundings and ourselves.

Silence turns us inward. In silence, we remain in intimate contact with our surroundings and ourselves. We rest in a state of inner clarity, an alert witness to the actions and feelings of everyone and everything around us.

The path of words uses the mind and intellect to achieve

---

3   Gems from Bhagavan, complied by Devaraja Mudaliar.

Part Four

understanding. Through the interaction of minds and the stimulation of the intellect new insight is gained. This is why Talmudic learning is traditionally done in pairs, because the Rabbis understood the power of two minds to inspire each other – to push each individual to new levels of insight and understanding.

Learning through silence is the path of the intuition, learning to hear the inner voice. One could say that silence is in fact another form of language; it is the language of pure consciousness. Sri Ramana Maharshi elucidates:

"Silence is never-ending speech ... For vocal speech, organs of speech are necessary and they precede speech. But the other speech lies even beyond thought. It is in short transcendent speech or unspoken words."[4]

Speech and silence then, are two methods of transmitting spiritual instruction.

Through speech and words we are able to access the world of ideas. Through listening to the words of great teachers and reading spiritual books, we expand our consciousness and gain new ways of perceiving and experiencing reality.

In silence, we touch the source of ideas – the supernal essence of Divine thought. The Baal Shem interprets the Rabbinic saying "a fence for wisdom is silence" to mean that when a person is silent, he can reach beyond the world of speech and thought and join himself to the world of wisdom from which all thought originates. Through silence we know a thing, not by analysis or formulation, but by a direct contact with its essence in the Mind of God.

Sri Ramana Maharshi asserts:

"Silence is the true spiritual instruction. It is the perfect spiritual instruction. It is suited only for the most advanced seeker. The others are unable to draw full inspiration from it. Therefore they require words to explain the Truth. But Truth is beyond words. It does not admit of explanation. All that is possible to do is only to indicate it. How is that to be done?"[5]

Speech uses the path of potent sound in prayer and ritual to approach God. Through the repetition of traditional formulations, we draw mind, heart and soul together and create a bond between spirit and matter. Through aspiration and positive thought, we

---

4   Munagala S. Venkataramiah, Talks with Sri Ramana Maharshi.
5   Venkataramiah, Talks.

align ourselves with our soul and establish an attuned resonance between our soul and personality.

The path of silence is about creating a space where God can enter. We remove the lower self and make place for the higher Self. We empty ourselves of all speech, thought and feeling and find God in the stillness that remains.

The medieval Christian saint, Saint John of the Cross, writes:

"It is better to learn to silence and quiet the faculties so that God may speak. For in this state ... the natural operations must fade from sight. This is realized when the soul arrives at solitude in these faculties, and God speaks to its heart, as the prophet (Hosea 2:14) asserts: 'Behold, I will allure her, and bring her into the wilderness, and speak tenderly to her.'"[6]

It is when the "normal faculties" have been quieted that this heart to heart talk can take place. Words or feelings only get in the way of the communication. They build a barrier between God and us. In silence, we go straight back to the source of our being and meet the living God that is there.

The Baal Shem saw the process of prayer as a progression from the path of words into the path of silence: words leading to sound leading to thought leading to Nothingness:

"In prayer you must put all your strength into the (pronunciation) of the words. And you shall go from letter to letter until you forget your physicality. And you think that the letters are combining and joining one to the other, and this is a great joy. If also in the material this is a joy, how much more so in the spirit. And this is the World of Formation. And afterwards you will come to the letters of thought and you will not hear what you are saying, and this is because you have come to the World of Creation. And then you come to the attribute of Nothingness – *Ayin*, that all your physical powers (senses) are annihilated, and this is the World of Emanation, the attribute of wisdom."

In Jewish tradition speech is the creative force. As Genesis 1:3 states: "And God said: let there be light, and there was light", and as Psalm 33:6 proclaims: "By the word of the Lord were the Heavens made."

---

6   Collected Works of St. John of the Cross, translated by Kieran Kavanaugh O.C.D. and Otilio Rodriguez O.C.D.

Part Four

Silence too is a powerful spiritual force. Once a devotee asked Sri Ramana Maharshi why he did not go about and preach the Truth to the people at large?

The Maharshi replied:

"How do you know that I am not doing it? Does preaching consist in mounting a platform and haranguing to the people around? Preaching is simple communication of knowledge. It may be done in Silence too.

"What do you think of a man listening to a harangue for an hour and going away without being impressed by it so as to change his life? Compare him with another who sits in a holy presence and leaves after some time with his outlook on life totally changed. Which is better: To preach loudly without effect or to sit silently sending forth intuitive forces to play on others?"[7]

Though both the path of words and the path of silence will take us towards God, ultimately, God is only heard in the stillness of interior silence. All the words of all the books and teachings of the world's religions cannot reveal the Lord to us. As Thayumanavar, a famous Indian saint once said: "Silence is the ocean in which all the rivers of all the religions discharge themselves."[8]

Or as the prophet Elijah discovered: God was not in the fire, nor the wind, nor in the earthquake but in the "still, small voice."

The Power Of Silence
Rabbi Dov Peretz Elkins

Sometimes the most eloquent thing we can say is nothing. Sometimes silence is the most powerful message one can convey.

In the High Holiday kaddish we add an extra word: *"Le-ayla"*. The phrase means that God is above – indeed far above (*le-ayla le-ayla*) all praise. All words are inadequate to praise God – even on Yom Kippur, the day when we say the most words of prayer. How ironic that on the High Holy Days, when we are more verbal in prayer than at any time of the year, we are reminded that words are so inadequate, by adding an extra word into the kaddish: *le-ayla* – so far above words and verbal praise is our God.

---

7 Venkataramiah, Talks.
8 Thayumanavar, Tamil poet and mystic.

The Sound Of Silence

When Aaron's two sons die, Moshe offers a few words of comfort (Lev. 10:3), but Aaron could do no more than sit in silence. Aaron is speechless. No words are adequate to express his grief. *Vayidom Aharon*! In two words the Torah describes the powerful emotional reaction that seized Aaron in this terrible and trying moment in his life.

We can all learn a lesson from Aaron. At the most heart-rending, the most painful, as well as during the most beautiful and uplifting moments in our life, silence is our most useful tool.

A teacher asked a class of seven-year-olds to write a paragraph about the most beautiful experience in their lives. One precocious child wrote on her paper: "The most beautiful experience in my life is too beautiful to put into words."

On a more sophisticated level, the science of General Semantics teaches that words are but maps of a territory. Words are not the territory. Sometimes we confuse our words with reality. They are only the maps that point to, or symbolize our reality. Words are sounds and vehicle, but they can be abused. Sometimes reality is too profound to be captured by words.

There are moments of affection between spouses, or between parents and children, which are too strong to be put into words. They may be expressed with a kiss, a hug, or with a meeting of the eyes. There are tender moments in our lives when words interfere with, instead of add to, our feelings.

There are moments in our lives when we appreciate great beauty, and we realize that no words can be found to express what we feel. When we stand on a high mountain; when we fly over a snow-capped mountain range, such as the Alps (as I have done). I can tell you that words would never have captured such sacred moments adequately for me. Whoever has stood at the top of Haifa Bay and looked down into the beautiful Mediterranean knows what I mean. Whoever has driven through the great rifts of the Negev, such as Machtesh Rimon; or witnessed a field of flowers, or sniffed some lilacs in Springtime. Whoever has peered into a sea of aging, wrinkled faces in a synagogue in Europe or Russia, blanketed with *talesim*, cannot put into words what she feels.

Whoever has seen the magic of a sunrise, or watched the golden glaze of the sun on the ocean, will understand the phrase "*Vayidom Aharon.*" Whoever has stood on the seashore in summer, or peered up at icicles on the trees in winter, will understand. Whoever has

Part Four

listened to a stirring symphony can hardly attempt to describe the inner emotions with the inadequate map of human words.

Even Shakespeare, the great artist and master wordsmith, acknowledged the superiority of silence over words when he wrote: "Silence is the most perfect herald of joy. I were but little happy if I could say how much."

There simply is no map large enough to cover the territory at such special moments. Our word symbols are woefully inadequate in trying to represent such deep feelings.

Moments of religious awe, what Heschel described as radical amazement, or the ineffable, are such special times. They resemble the moment when God communicated with our ancestors at Mt. Sinai. The record of that Divine-human encounter is inscribed in the two tablets of the Ten Commandments. But the actual encounter itself could not be captured in language. The midrash (on Exodus 20) tells us that "no bird sang, no fowl flew, no ox bellowed, no angel stirred a wing ... the sea did not roar and no creature spoke. The whole world stood hushed into breathless silence and the Voice went forth and proclaimed "I am Adonai your God." The world of nature stood still, and the Israelites at the bottom of the mountain were standing in hushed silence. Only the voice of the Creator was adequate for such a moment.

Our ancestors knew the power of silence. We are told that the Hasidim Rishonim would sit in silence for a whole hour readying themselves for prayer. Maimonides, the greatest philosopher of the Middle Ages, suggested that God might never have commanded us to offer sacrifices or utter words of prayer but for the fact that we are mortal and incapable of staying on the high level of silence and contemplation for a prolonged period of time.

Our Siddur is aware that words are woefully inadequate in trying to pray. In the *Nishmat* prayer we recite each Shabbat morning: "Were our mouth filled with song as the sea, and our tongue with ringing praise as the roaring waves; were our lips full of adoration as the wide expanse of heaven; and our eyes sparkling like the sun or the moon; we would still be unable to thank and bless God's name."

In the kaddish we recite many times every day that God's praise is *"le-ayla min kol birkhata ve-shirata"* – far above any blessing or song which we mortals could possibly utter. And, in fact, on the high holidays, we go even further, as we pointed out before. We add another word to every form of the kaddish, when we say that God is "*le-ayla ule-ayla*" far, far above any words of praise we could create in the most beautiful poem in the world.

The Age of Noise Pollution

We live in an age when unending, blaring noises surround us and shatter our nerves. It may be automobiles in the street below, or airplanes cutting across the sky above; it may be the computer printer, or the fax machine, or simply the telephone. In today's technologically advanced world we are plagued with additional noises – the ubiquitous beeper, or the cellular phone, which rings even in synagogue when all is quiet and sacred, and the noise of the outside world bursts in like a thief, stealing our calm and robbing our soul of its peace.

We are so accustomed to these noises that we no longer know how to sit in silence, and think or meditate. The late Norman Cousins wrote: "Plainly this is not an age of the meditative man. It is a squinting, sprinting, shoving age. Substitutes for repose are a million dollar business. Silence, already a nation's most critical shortage, is almost a nasty word. Modern man may or may not be obsolete, but he is certainly wired for sound."

It is, no doubt, this proclivity to wordiness and verbosity that led the great sage Rabban Gamliel to teach his famous aphorism in Pirke Avot: "All my days I have grown up among the sages and have found nothing better for a person than silence."

"Silence," said the famous teacher Rabbi Akiva, "is a fence to wisdom."

Our Hasidic masters understood very well the power of silence in the development of the spiritual life, and the dangers of the intrusion of noise into the attempt to feel God's presence. Rabbi Nachman of Bratslav taught that whoever does not reserve one hour each day to be alone in silence is not human. He also said: "As children we learn to speak; as elders we learn silence. And this is the great flaw we have: that we learn to speak before we learn to be quiet." For that reason the most beautiful songs of the Hasidic tradition are the *niggunim,* the songs without words. Songs which just hum with "la-la-la," or "Bim-bam" or "oy-vey" or other made-up sounds. Sounds that are not words, but vessels which can capture any feeling that bubbles up from the heart of the worshiper.

Part Four

Rabbi Baruch Silverstein told the story about a visit to Israel when he led a pilgrimage of members of his congregation. He tells of his colorful and loquacious guide. Like all of Israel's guides he was knowledgeable, entertaining, and full of stories and history. Israel's well-trained tour guides are intelligent and articulate; talkative and glib. During this particular tour the guide was especially gifted in his ability to describe the sites and scenes of Eretz Yisrael. He lectured to the group on history, philosophy, geography, archeology, economics, politics and military strategy.

When the group arrived at the Kotel, however, he led them out of the bus, and remained standing in the back without uttering a word. During the entire stay at the Kotel, not a word from this normally talkative teacher. When everyone returned to the bus, Rabbi Silverstein asked him about this unusual behavior. The guide replied: "At the special training school for guides we are repeatedly warned not to say anything at the Western Wall. At the Kotel, he said, with obvious emotion, the tourist must listen not to the guide's voice but to higher voices, to greater voices, to the voice of Jewish history, to the 'still small voice' of God."

Silence and Solitude Require Practice

If we want to find the deep inner space in our heart where we meet God, and we meet our true inner self, we need to discipline ourselves to learn how to be quiet. How to listen. How to stop the mental chatter that goes on all the time. To turn off the TV, and just sit quietly and slow down our mind. It is worth the effort.

For many in this age of spiritual search, a Retreat, or a Shabbaton, is an experience to find the quiet we are speaking of. It is an opportunity to flee from the noise, the hustle-bustle of the city, the treadmill of our work, and become reacquainted with our soul. With the open spaces of nature. To learn how to stop the commotion inside our head, and rest our tongues as well as our ears. Just to contemplate; to think; to rediscover the power of silence. It does not come easily at first. It takes practice and discipline, like all worthy endeavors. But it is surely worth the time and effort it takes.

In a wonderful book of advice called *Letters To My Son* (New World Library, 1993) Kent Nerburn writes about silence and solitude:

The Sound Of Silence

"It is worth the struggle. Slowly, inexorably, we emerge into the ultimate quiet of solitude.

"We are in a place where we are beyond thoughts – where we hear each sound and feel each heartbeat; where we are present to each change of sunlight on the earth around us, and we live in the awareness of the ongoing presence of life.

"In this awareness the whole world changes around us. A tree ceases to be an object and becomes a living thing. We can smell its richness, hear its rustlings, sense its rhythms. Silence becomes a symphony. Time changes from a series of moments strung together to a seamless motion riding on the rhythms of the stars.

"Solitude is a place you reach, not a decision you make."

Silence as the Way to God

For those of us who pretend to be searchers for the spiritual life, to seek to find the true God wherever the Presence may be hiding from us, we need to look in one more place. In the hushed silence of our stilled heart.

Rabbi Sidney Greenberg teaches us that "Daily the prayer book reminds us that we can worship God not only with 'the words of my mouth' but also with 'the meditations of my heart.' I need not shout my faith. Thrice eloquent are quiet trees and the green listening sod; hushed are the stars, whose power is never spent; the hills are mute. Yet how they speak of God!"

It is in this kind of silence and wonder that we begin to understand ourselves, the world, and God. Through it we are better able to know who we are, where we are, and what are our true tasks here on earth.

The Biblical prophet Habakkuk said it many centuries ago (2:20):

Adonai is in the Holy Temple.
Let all the earth keep silence in God's Presence!

Amen!

Glossary

Al Chet – The confessional service said on Yom Kippur; many of the sins listed are related to speech.

Amidah – Also called *Shemona Esray,* the main section of morning, afternoon, and evening prayers.

Avak Leshon Hara – The residue of evil speech.

Chavurat Resha – An evil grouping.

Chazal – Jewish sages of the Mishna, Tosefta and Talmud eras.

Chesed – Kindness.

Chillul Hashem – Desecrating God's name.

Chofetz Chaim – The book, published in 1873, written by Rabbi Israel Meir Kagan Hakohen of Radin, dealing with the laws of guarding one's speech. The name *Chofetz Chaim* is inspired from a verse in Psalms, "Whoever of you desires life", and from this work, the Rabbi became known as the *Chofetz Chaim*.

Dibbur Peh – The spewing of hateful words.

Halacha (Halachot) – Jewish laws.

Kiddush Hashem – Sanctifying God's name.

Leshon Hara (*loshen hore,* Yiddish) – Evil speech; slander, gossip, put-downs, vilification of any kind – a nasty, evil, and pernicious act that can destroy a reputation and ruin a life.

Leshon Hatov – The verbal affirmation of another person, the careful use of words which the Jewish tradition implies when it warns us about the sins of speech.

Metzora – The person afflicted with *tzaraat*.

Midrash – The interpretive collection on Biblical writings.

Medaber – The one who speaks.

Motzi shem ra – Speech which is negative and untrue.

Musar Movement – The 19th century effort to center people's attention on ethical responsibilities, led by Rabbi Israel Salanter.

Ner Tamid – Eternal light.
Neshamah – One's soul.
Rechilut – Talebearing; lit. peddler.

Sinat Chinam – Gratuitous hatred; a key feature is the use of derogatory language.
Shmirat Halashon – Guarding one's speech.

Talmid Hacham – Torah Scholar.
Teshuva – expiation for one's misdeed.
Toelet – *Leshon Hara* that may be repeated for a constructive purpose.
Tumah – Ritual impurity; a spiritual state that prevents a person from participating in the worship life of the community.
Tzaraat (*Tzaraas*)– A skin affliction, the physical manifestation of a spiritual or ritual problem; Biblical leprosy.

Vidui – Confession.

Yetzer Hara – Evil inclination.
Yetzer Hatov – Good inclination.

www.ingramcontent.com/pod-product-compliance
Lightning Source LLC
Chambersburg PA
CBHW071722090426
42738CB00009B/1848